TRUMPET
CALL TO
WOMEN

Other books by the same author:

Reflections on the Baptism in the Holy Spirit
Reflections on the Gifts of the Spirit
Reflections on a Song of Love (1 Corinthians 13)

In course of preparation:

Consider Him (Twelve Qualities of Christ)
Battle for the Body
The Clash of Tongues (1 Corinthians 14)

A TRUMPET CALL TO WOMEN

HUGH B. BLACK

NEW DAWN BOOKS

GREENOCK, SCOTLAND

© Hugh B. Black 1988

First published 1988 by
NEW DAWN BOOKS
27 Denholm Street, Greenock PA16 8RH, Scotland

ISBN 1 870944 03 8

Unless otherwise stated biblical quotations are
from the Revised Version

Cover photo: Craig Richardson

Production and printing in England for

NEW DAWN BOOKS

27 Denholm Street, Greenock PA16 8RH, Scotland
by Nuprint Ltd, Harpenden, Herts AL5 4SE.

Contents

Acknowledgements

I am grateful to all those who continue to encourage me to write; to my daughters, Dr Alison H. Black for editorial assistance and Mrs Grace Gault for help with Greek references; to Mrs Black, Miss Jennifer Jack and Mr Alastair Duff for proof-reading and helpful advice; and to Miss Irene Morrison for laborious work in processing the various drafts of the book.

My thanks are also due to the authors and publishers whose works have been quoted. I am indebted to the late Professor William Barclay, Rev. John Stott, and particularly to Dr James B. Hurley, whose *Men and Women in Biblical Perspective* provided many valuable insights. After my own book was written and at the printer's, I discovered Dr Gordon D. Fee's *The First Epistle to the Corinthians*, published in *The New International Commentary on the New Testament* series (general editor F. F. Bruce). I have managed to make reference to this work in the notes. Since Dr Fee's book was first published in 1987, this will give readers access to some of the most recent scholarship in this field.

Foreword

I would like it to be known that the contribution of the Foreword to this book is no mere formality. Its subject is one of considerable importance to myself, having been involved over a period of approximately forty years and especially during the last twenty years in public preaching and teaching and the operation of the ministries and gifts of the Spirit. When the call of God came, I was not at that stage prepared to launch out into public life, but through the encouragement given by the writer I was persuaded to accept the call to public ministry, particularly in the propagation of Pentecost as in Acts 2. Having worked in partnership over a long period of years, I have a very clear understanding of the author's attitude on the subject and endorse his conclusions with pleasure and enthusiasm.

Elizabeth H. Taylor

Preface

There are few more controversial subjects facing the Church in our day than that of women ministry.

For the liberal wing of the Church, which regards the Bible as giving guidelines rather than imposing age-abiding standards, there may be no great problems. The role of women then and now may be regarded as reflecting the cultures of different periods of history. Change may be both expected and welcomed.

But for Christians who regard the Bible as authoritative for both doctrine and practice, the position is very different. There are millions who view the Bible as Divinely and fully inspired, and are anxious to abide closely by its teaching. To many of these, the subject of women ministry causes real problems. Many shades of opinion are reflected amongst them. Some see women in an almost silent role so far as ministry is concerned. Others believe that the New Testament teaches that women do have a vocal role, although a limited one. Others take the view that in all senses women are equal to men in spiritual matters. This school acknowledges that there are restrictions on women, but these are seen as related to natural relationships with men.

There are Scriptures which at least on the surface seem

to support all these positions. Is reconciliation of the appropriate parts possible? Is there a clear solution which meets all the difficulties? In my view, a very strong case can be made for the last position: that is, that in all senses women are equal to men in spiritual matters.

In the second part of the book there is a testimony from a lady who has been deeply used in the work of God for many years. Her experience will be an encouragement to others.

PART I
THE SCRIPTURAL CASE

Introduction

This is the fifth book in a series. These are: *Reflections on the Baptism in the Holy Spirit, Reflections on the Gifts of the Spirit, Reflections on a Song of Love (1 Cor 13)*, and *The Clash of Tongues (1 Cor 14)*, due to be published later. The present book follows naturally from the commentary on 1 Corinthians 14, where the main part of the chapter deals with the regulation of spiritual gifts. Verses 34–36 seem to be almost an interjection, and indeed the verses are found in different contexts in some of the ancient manuscripts. It seemed reasonable, therefore, to extract these verses and deal with them separately. In addition, a consideration of them opens the whole field of women ministry, and I feel that this is of such vital importance and contemporary relevance that it should have a book to itself.

I personally strongly favour women ministry in a very wide sense. This derives from a study of the Bible and perhaps particularly from a consideration of deep underlying Scriptural principles which are not always immediately apparent on a surface reading. It also derives from a lifetime of experience of observing the deep working of God through women.

While strongly emphasising certain positive aspects of

the case, I have tried to be honest in facing the difficulties which some of the texts present. The debate does not centre on the fact of women ministry so much as on its extent, and specifically on whether there are any areas closed to women which are open to men. I leave the reader to judge my conclusions.

The work falls into a number of natural sections. The position of women is examined in both the natural and spiritual dimensions, with particular reference to Eden, the period of the patriarchs and prophets, the era prior to Christ, Christ's own day, and the early Church age.

1

With Eve in Eden

I remember, as a student, being intrigued and somewhat puzzled by a remark of the late Professor Stones of the Chair of Medieval History in Glasgow University. He indicated that there were really comparatively few major events or issues in history and that these should receive our main concentration. It seemed to me as a somewhat embroiled student that there was an endless succession of complicated matters requiring to be unravelled and understood. The trees hid the wood. With more mature years I can now understand what the professor meant. In the history of our land there were key issues—events which in some cases affected whole nations and some-times future generations, e.g. the coming of the Angles, Saxons and Jutes; the Roman and Viking invasions; the Norman Conquest; the Scottish War of Independence; the Renaissance; the Reformation; the Union of 1707; the Napoleonic Wars; the First and Second World Wars.

In the history portrayed in the Bible a similar pattern can be seen. There were major and sometimes world-significant events, e.g. the Fall of man; the Flood; the call of Abram; the Exodus from Egypt; the giving of the Law; the founding of the monarchy; various captivities;

the advent of Christ; the impact of Paul. With the first of these we are presently concerned.

For many years I have found the story of Eden fascinating. As in that other garden, Gethsemane, there are unseen depths which are beyond our easy plumbing, but some degree of plumbing is necessary to understand the role of Eve as woman and particularly as woman in relation to man; and this is the subject of our enquiry.

Adam and Eve were created male and female in the image and likeness of God.[1] They were given dominion over the rest of creation and were intended to multiply and replenish the earth. It is clear that Adam was first made and that since it was not good for him to dwell alone, Eve was made to be his helpmeet. Adam was created from the dust but Eve was made from a rib of Adam. Adam was not made for Eve, as we read in Paul's writings, but the woman was made for the man. He was first created and that in the image of God; she was later created and that in the image of man. It is for this reason that Paul later instructed the Corinthians that in a Christian assembly, women should have their heads covered. Man should be uncovered because, being in the image of God, he reflected the glory of God, but the woman, being in the image of man, reflected the glory of man and no such glory was to be reflected in the presence of God. Only God's glory was to shine there.

Now in the Trinity, we read that there is equality, for example, between the Father and the Son and yet headship is vested in the Father. Our first parents were made in the image of God and while there was a headship vested in the man there is no suggestion of any inequality between them in the beginning. The trouble comes later. With the Fall a very different situation arises. The possibility of becoming better was suggested to Eve. To accept

18

the suggestion would probably appeal to her natural curiosity. All would be shrouded in that strange fascination which is so often associated with the masquerading 'angel of light'. It is salutary to remember that it is sin to be deceived. We never need be and are accountable if we are. Eve was deceived by the serpent and sinned. Adam was not deceived but deliberately took of the fruit from Eve and shared her fall. It is interesting to speculate as to whether he could have saved his wife from the consequences of her action if he had remained true to God, or whether she would have gone down alone. What then would the consequences to Adam have been? Perhaps another C. S. Lewis will arise to write another *Perelandra* based on such an assumption. Another interesting speculation relates to the degree of guilt. Since the sin of Adam was deliberate, was not his the greater guilt? And yet the Bible does not seem to give that impression—at least on a superficial reading.

The judgment of God quickly falls on all three participants in the tragedy: Adam, Eve and the serpent. The relevant part for our present purpose is contained in these words relative to Eve: 'Thy desire shall be to thy husband and he shall rule over thee.'[2] This is quite new and is a direct consequence of the Fall. It is not related to the original plan of God for the man and the woman. Note, we are not told whether this is a punishment on Eve for her sin or simply a natural consequence of it.

In the beginning God planned for a perfect man and woman to found a perfect race and inhabit the earth. In that plan there is no suggestion of one ruling the other. They would both have a perfect relationship with God which would preclude a certain type of dominion and subjection. They would perfectly fulfil their complementary roles and form a unity. They were created as spiritual beings to have a relationship with God but they were also created to have an earth life. At that stage there was no conflict between the two. The life on earth and the life in God were in no way incompatible. There was no division between the natural and the spiritual as we know it today and as it was so clearly defined by Paul:

> For I delight in the law of God after the inward man: but I see a different law in my members, warring against the law of my mind, and bringing me into captivity under the law of sin which is in my members (Rom 7:22–23).

The division came as soon as sin came into the garden. Now it is important to take stock at this point. Both Adam and Eve had a responsibility to God and to each other. They had their own individual spiritual lives and their lives in relationship to each other in the natural world. It is the second of these that God regulates by giving man dominion over the woman. In the spiritual sphere there is no such provision.

Before leaving Eden it is not only interesting but perhaps essential for our later study of this subject to ponder what the original plan of God was for our race. In Eden we see our first parents in a condition of innocency. Was that God's permanent eternal plan for them? I think not. There was a forbidden tree in the garden. It faced them with a choice—the choice of obedience or disobedience. It formed a basis on which Satan could operate. Now God not only had foreknowledge of this but He allowed it. May He not indeed have planned it so that man might be tested as the last Adam was in another garden and given the opportunity to resist evil and pass from untested innocency to chosen holiness— indeed to take the whole race up to a higher plane where they could enjoy the fruit of the tree of endless life? It was to take a greater than Adam to make the right choice, which Christ did in Gethsemane, and by way of a cursed tree to give His followers the right to eat of the tree of Life.

To sum up: Adam and Eve had been created equal but his was the headship. Initially there was no division between spiritual and natural life and no problems of dominion or submission, but with the coming of sin the woman in things natural was placed in subjection to man. In things spiritual she retained her own identity before God and was not made dependent on man or answerable to him. To put the position in clear terms: her spiritual position was identical to that envisaged by Paul in a later day when he gave instruction to Christian women with unbelieving husbands in 1 Corinthians 5:15. An unbelieving husband was envisaged as leaving his wife: there is no suggestion that the wife in such a case should renounce Christ to have her husband remain. The teaching of Christ further supports the view:

> He that loveth father or mother more than me is not worthy of me: and he that loveth son or daughter more than me is not worthy of me (Mt 10:37–39).

This underlines the same principle—the demands of God are paramount and supersede all human relationships. God expects His every follower to put Him first regardless of all other claims. No less a demand was made of Eve and all other women. Their ultimate loyalty was ever to be to God. The relationship was always direct and never through the man. Through the ages this has not changed.

Two distinct spheres are identifiable—the natural and

the spiritual. In the first the man had dominion over the woman; in the second there is no such arrangement. Woman is forever free and directly responsible to God. We will find that this principle can be traced throughout the whole Bible and it will clearly emerge from chapter to chapter in this book.

Notes

[1] In being part of man, Eve may be regarded as being in the image of God in a general sense. She was, however, in the image of man in a particular sense. See further p. 57, n. 3.

[2] James B. Hurley argues that the woman's desire here means desire to rule her husband—something in which she would not be successful. He maintains that the post-Eden position did not reflect a fundamental change in the existing hierarchical relationship, but was rather a distortion of this. See Hurley, *Man and Woman in Biblical Perspective* (Inter-Varsity Press, 1981), p. 219.

2

In the Days of the Patriarchs and Prophets

The period from the coming of judgment on our first parents to the end of the Old Testament, may be divided into two sections in our examination of the role of woman in society generally and, more particularly, her position relative to man and to God:

—the days of the patriarchs;
—the age of the law and the prophets.

During the first period women are seen as occupying an honoured place. They had their own clear identity and role. The patriarchs undoubtedly led their tribal groups and had authority over them—but their wives were no mere chattels. Sarah, Rebekah, Rachel, Leah were all women of character and their position was respected by their husbands. It should be noted too that while the wives were under the authority of their husbands in things temporal they also had their own relationship with God. This can be seen clearly in the case of Sarah. When God promised a son she laughed and had direct communication with Him in denying her laughter. (Gen 18:15). Rachel rejoiced that God had heard her when her handmaid bore a son (Gen 30:6). Hagar had very direct dealing with God during her flight from Sarah (Gen 16:7–14).

In short the principle which we observed in the last chapter is seen outworked here. In things temporal the man has authority over the woman. In things spiritual she is her own agent and has direct communication with God without reference to the man. She is not seen, however, in a matriarchal or priestly role. Neither then nor at any other time is she seen using the sacrificial knife. This, in the era we next consider, became the function of the Levites—not the function of men as distinct from women—but the function of a select group of people chosen for that purpose.

With the coming of the law many matters were regulated and from that time, through the days of the prophets, the position of woman may be summarised as follows:

She could inherit property. In Numbers 27:1–11 we read of the daughters of Zelophehad who appealed to Moses regarding their inheritance. God gave him clear commandment that the inheritance of their dead father was to pass to them and then He gave a statute of inheritance which covered all such cases.

She could transact business. Of the virtuous woman in Proverbs 31:16 we read: 'She considereth a field, and buyeth it.'

She could take part in government. Of Deborah we read in Judges 4:4–6 'Now Deborah, a prophetess, the wife of Lappidoth, she judged Israel at that time. And she dwelt under the palm tree of Deborah . . . and the children of Israel came up to her for judgment. And she sent and called Barak . . . and said unto him, Hath not the Lord, the God of Israel, commanded, saying,

Go . . . .' Deborah was a judge to whom Israelites willingly submitted.

In the case of Athaliah we read that for six years she reigned (although perhaps wrongly) as monarch over the land (2 Kings 11:3). There is no condemnation of her, however, for holding office on the grounds that she was a woman.

She is found in the role of prophet. In Exodus 15:20–21 we read, 'And Miriam the prophetess, the sister of Aaron, took a timbrel in her hand; and all the women went out after her with timbrels and with dances. And Miriam answered them, Sing ye to the Lord, for he hath triumphed gloriously; the horse and his rider has he thrown into the sea.'

In Judges 4:4 we have noted: 'Now Deborah, a prophetess, the wife of Leppidoth, she judged Israel at that time.'

In 2 Kings 22:14–20, Huldah the prophetess gave a very clear word from God relative to the land and its inhabitants and king. King Josiah sent five dignitaries to her to enquire as to what God would do about the nation's fearful disobedience to the law. She gave the word of God on the matter and her role of prophetess was obviously recognised. The king himself received her word.

Women had a right and indeed a duty to come to the tabernacle and later to the temple to worship, to fulfil vows and to offer sacrifices. In Deuteronomy 31:10–12, people—men, women and children—assembled to listen to the public readings of the law. The women were included.

And Moses commanded them, saying, At the end of every seven years, in the set time of the year of release, in the feast of tabernacles, when all Israel is come to appear before the Lord thy God in the place which he shall choose, thou shalt read this law before all Israel in their hearing. Assemble the people, the men and the women and the little ones, and thy stranger that is within thy gates, that they may hear, and that they may learn, and fear the Lord your God, and observe to do all the words of this law.

In 1 Samuel 1:24 Hannah is seen bringing the sacrifice in the year she brought Samuel to Eli. In cases of purification women brought their own sacrifices to the priests (Lev 12:6, 15:29).

In short, all Israel were enjoined to love and serve God: the women were part of the covenant community with full responsibility to fulfil these functions.

The participation of women, however, went beyond the hearing and obeying of the law generally, the fulfilling of vows and the bringing of sacrifices. They approached God in prayer, e.g. Rebekah (Gen 25:22), Rachel (Gen 30:6, 22) and Hannah (1 Sam 1:1–10)— and their prayers were answered (Gen 25:33; 30:6, 22). Indeed His angel appeared to them and dealt with them personally (Gen 16:7–14, Judg 13:39). Throughout the period women appear in distinguished roles, e.g. Hannah, Abigail, Naomi, Ruth and Esther.

In the case of Hannah there was clearly a very deep and personal relationship with God. Indeed she seems to have had an intimacy with Him unknown to her husband. She prayed for a son and dedicated the unborn Samuel to God. Her prayer was wonderfully answered. Abigail was a wise woman and she showed no foolish deference to her churlish husband, Nabal, when his life was in danger from David and his men. Naomi learned wisdom with experience and demonstrated a real knowledge of God and his ways. Ruth beautifully and sweetly fitted into the congregation of Israel, having personally chosen Naomi's God and people. Esther was a true queen. She stood where no man of Israel was able to stand in a dark hour in the history of the nation. Through her action the hour was transformed to one of light and victory.

Women sang in the choirs as did men. We read:

—of a group of women who 'served at the door of the tent of meeting' (Ex 38:8);

—of three daughters of Heman who with their brothers were 'under the hands of their father for song in the House of the Lord, with cymbals, psalteries and harps, for the service of the house of God' (2 Chron 25:5–6);

—'and all the singing men and singing women spake of Josiah in their lamentations' (2 Chron 35:25).

Perhaps the description of a virtuous woman in Proverbs 31:10–31 sums up the way in which the woman was ideally regarded in Old Testament times. So far as the home sphere was concerned the principle ran true: the relationship established by God after the Fall was maintained. Her desire in things natural was to her husband. She was subject to him. The outworking of the principle on the spiritual side was also maintained. Hannah, Abigail, Naomi, Ruth and Esther all enjoyed personal relationships with God which were direct and in no way dependent on men.

3

Woman's Nadir

The next period with which we have to deal shows a marked change in the role and position of women.

The world into which Christ was to be born would have been almost unrecognisable to Moses, David or Isaiah. Gone were the days of open, free worship with their emphasis on mercy, righteousness and judgment— the weightier matters of the law to which Christ later referred in dealing with the Pharisees. Rigid legalism was the order of the day, Mint, anise and cummin were indeed tithed and the outsides of platters rigorously cleansed. The whited sepulchres, as Christ described them, were no doubt gleaming bright but nevertheless they were charnel houses inside full of dead men's bones.

A dark day had dawned and a new and harsh order arrived. This is not too difficult to understand. Between the Old and New Testament much had befallen the Jewish nation:—many were in exile; the Jews of the Dispersion were numerous; the land was occupied by the Romans; foreign influences had affected social custom and altered the way in which women were viewed; regarded as generally less intelligent than men, they were also seen as a source of sexual temptation; the woman's role in social life had greatly diminished; her place in worship and ministry was also altered under Judaism; she could attend worship but was not required to do so except on particular occasions; she could not lead in worship; even the oral reading of Scripture was no longer regarded as being suitable for her; most rabbis would not for a moment have considered teaching a woman; the Talmud, a collection of Jewish writings dating from before Christ to the 6th century AD, classified women with slaves and heathen and assumed them incapable of learning.

The contempt with which women were regarded in the ancient world generally is difficult for us to fathom today. Plato, who believed in reincarnation, considered that 'a bad man's fate would be reincarnation as a woman.'[1] Aristotle regarded a woman as a kind of mutilated man: 'Females are imperfect males, accidentally produced by the father's inadequacy or by the malign influence of a moist south wind.'[2] It might have been expected that the Jews with their religious background would have withstood the influence of Greece and Rome—but not only were non-Christian Jews affected, the Church fathers too were influenced. Amongst the former Josephus, a contemporary of Paul, wrote, 'The woman is inferior to the man in every way.'[3] One rabbi, Jose ben Johana (c.150 BC), has been quoted as saying: 'He that talks much with women brings evil on himself . . . and at last will inherit Gehenna.'[4] The Mishnah in discussing situations where women could be divorced without recompense included the following: going out with hair unbound, spinning in the street and speaking with a man.

In the Apocryphal book of Ecclesiasticus (c.190 BC) ben Sirach wrote:

Any spite rather than the spite of woman! . . .
I would sooner keep house with a lion or a dragon
   than keep house with a spiteful wife . . .
No wickedness comes anywhere near the wickedness of a
woman,
   may a sinner's lot be hers! . . .
Low spirits, gloomy face, stricken heart:
   such the achievements of a spiteful wife . . .
Sin began with a woman,
   and thanks to her we all must die.
Do not let water find a leak,
   do not allow a spiteful woman free rein for her tongue.
If she will not do as you tell her,
   get rid of her.[5]

Philo, a contemporary of Paul, distinguishes between men and women as follows: 'the attitude of man is informed by reason, [that] of woman by sensuality.'[6] James B. Hurley observes:

> In Philo and in Josephus we have something which we did not find in the Old Testament or even in ben Sirach; we find an explicit teaching of intrinsic female inferiority.[7]

Commenting on the Talmud's frequent classification of women with children and slaves. James Hurley quotes the notorious statement of Rabbi Judah ben Alai (c.AD 150):

> A man is bound to say the following three blessings daily: '[Blessed art thou . . .] who has not made me a heathen', ' . . . who hast not made me a woman', ' . . . and who has not made me a brutish man'.[8]

As William Barclay comments,

> In the Jewish form of morning prayer . . . a Jewish man

every morning gave thanks that God had not made him 'a Gentile, a slave or a woman'. . . . In Jewish law a woman was not a person, but a thing. She had no legal rights whatsoever; she was absolutely in her husband's possession to do with as he willed.[9]

With the kind of attitude displayed here, Deborah and Huldah presented real problems to the Rabbis. Hurley comments:

Deborah comes up for mention only four times in the Talmud. On the two occasions in which she received more than a passing mention, she is depreciated for boasting and for haughtiness. Huldah's role as prophetess is a problem, as she lived while there were male prophets alive. How could Josiah have sent for a word from God through Huldah instead of through Jeremiah? Answers suggested range from the suggestion that she was a relative of Jeremiah's and that he did not mind, to the suggestion that he had gone to retrieve the ten lost tribes and was not around. The second mention of Huldah is found in an interesting anecdote which more or less sums up the rabbis' attitude toward women in public roles:

Rabbi Nahman said: Haughtiness does not befit women. There were two haughty women, and their names are hateful, one being called a hornet [literal meaning of Deborah] and the other a weasel [literal meaning of Huldah]. Of the hornet it is written, *And she sent and called Barak*, instead of going to him. Of the weasel it is written, *Say to the man*, instead of 'Say to the king [Josiah]'

Rabbi Nahman objected to these two prophetesses taking roles of authority as they spoke in the Lord's name. Women directing men were out of place for him.'[10]

31

From Genesis Rabbah 18:2 the following quotation is illuminating:

> [God] considered well from what part he would create her. Said He: 'I will not create her from [Adam's] head lest she be swell-headed; nor from the eye, lest she be a coquette; nor from the ear, lest she be an eavesdropper; nor from the mouth, lest she be a gossip; nor from the heart, lest she be prone to jealousy; nor from the hand, lest she be light-fingered; nor from the foot, lest she be a gadabout; but from the modest part of man, for even when he stands naked, that part is covered.' And as He created each limb He ordered her, 'Be a modest woman.' Yet in spite of all this, *But ye have set at nought all my counsel, and would none of my reproof* (Prov 1:25). I did not create her from the head, but she is swell-headed . . ; nor from the eye, yet she is a coquette . . ; nor from the ear, yet she is an eavesdropper . . ; nor from the heart, yet she is prone to jealousy . . . ; nor from the hand, yet she is light-fingered . . ; nor from the foot, yet she is a gadabout . . . .[11]

The intemperate language of Tertullian, one of the early Church fathers, falls strangely on our ears today:

> You [women] are the devil's gateway; you are the unsealer of that (forbidden) tree; you are the first deserter of the divine law; you are she who persuaded him whom the devil was not valiant enough to attack. You destroyed so easily God's image, man. On account of your desert—that is, death—even the Son of God had to die.[12]

One other aspect of life in this era should be considered before closing the section: marriage and divorce. Marriage was instituted by God in Eden. It was an honourable estate which had the Divine blessing. Initially it was viewed as lifelong and while polygamy was practised from an early date, divorce was not. Because of the hardness of the hearts of the Israelites the latter was ultimately permitted—but as Christ said, 'From the beginning it was not so.' Now the Mosaic Law governing divorce is found in Deuteronomy 24:1–4 and differences of interpretation of the passage had very important consequences.

Before looking closely at the subject as it affected Jews it is salutary and somewhat shocking to study the attitude of the Romans to divorce. To be free of a wife a man merely had to tell her to go. There was no need for a formal legal process. As we noticed earlier a woman was regarded almost as a thing rather than a person; she had no legal rights at all. Divorce was extremely common. In this connection Barclay writes in *Ethics in a Permissive Society*:[13]

> Martial tells of a woman who was living with her tenth husband. Juvenal tells of a woman who had eight husbands in five years. And Jerome tells us of what must have been the unsurpassable record, the case of a woman who was married to her twenty-third husband, she being his twenty-first wife.

Seneca said that women were married to be divorced and were divorced to be married.[14]

To return to the Jewish world, much depended on the interpretation of the words in Deuteronomy:

> When a man taketh a wife, and marrieth her, then it shall be, if she find no favour in his eyes, because he hath found some unseemly thing in her, that he shall write her a bill of divorcement, and give it in her hand, and send her out of his house. (Deut 24:1).

The words 'unseemly thing' were critical. Shammai, one of the great authorities, taught that serious uncleanness was the only permissible ground of divorce. Hillel, the other most famous teacher, however, taught that 'unseemly thing' could mean 'going out with her hair unbound, spinning in the street, talking to another man, spoiling his dinner, speaking disrespectfully to her husband's parents in her husband's presence, becoming a scolding woman.'[15] Many in Israel preferred to follow the teaching of Hillel to that of Shammai.

It was into this world that Christ was born. Never in any age had women been so downtrodden and treated with such contempt. They were lightly married and lightly divorced and that without redress or recompense. They were often treated as chattels rather than persons. With no legal rights in society they were also excluded from active participation in worship. They were not considered worthy to be taught the things of God.

For many years as I have conducted marriage ceremonies I have emphasised the debt which women owe to Christ but never until writing this chapter have I realised how very great it really is. The darkest hour may indeed have been just before the dawn. Not only were Zebulun and Naphtali to see a great light—so were the women of Israel and ultimately the women of all the world who would come under the power of the gospel.

Notes

[1] John Stott, *Issues Facing Christians Today* (Marshall Morgan & Scott, 1984), p.235.
[2] Quoted *ibid*.
[3] Quoted in James B. Hurley, 'Women in ministry,' in Shirley

Lees, ed., *The Role of Women* (Inter-Varsity Press, 1984), p.125.

[4] Quoted *ibid*.

[5] Ecclus 25:13–26. Quoted from the Jerusalem Bible by Hurley, *Man and Woman in Biblical Perspective*, p.60.

[6] Quoted in Hurley, *ibid*., p.61.

[7] *Ibid*., p.62.

[8] *Ibid*.

[9] Stott, *op. cit*., p.235.

[10] Hurley, *Man and Woman in Biblical Perspective*, p.70.

[11] *Ibid*., p.74.

[12] Quoted in Stott, *op. cit*., p.235.

[13] William Barclay, *Ethics in a Permissive Society* (Collins Fontana Books, 1971), p.198.

[14] *Ibid*.

[15] *Ibid*., p.199.

4

In the Days of His Flesh

There is a lovely curtain raiser to this section. It is as though a bird sang ere dawn broke. Despite the restrictions regarding women in the temple and in the synagogues, we read:

> And there was one Anna, a prophetess, the daughter of Phanuel, of the tribe of Asher (she was of a great age, having lived with a husband seven years from her virginity. And she had been a widow even for fourscore and four years), which departed not from the temple, worshipping with fastings and supplications night and day. And coming up at that very hour she gave thanks unto God, and spake of him to all them that were looking for the redemption of Jerusalem (Lk 2:36–39).

No law kept her out of the temple and certainly no Judaistic attitude to women or rabbinical interpretation bound her spirit. She was in touch with the living God. She was a prophetess and her being female in no way inhibited her communion with her God. Surely this early incident was a portent of good things to come.

We have observed the kind of world into which Christ was born and the place it afforded women. There is a danger of taking many things for granted through long familiarity with basic facts and sometimes failing to see the wonder of the changes Christ made. His attitude to women and the way He treated them was radically different from the custom of His age.

Where religious leaders considered synagogue instruction as being exclusively for men (some rabbis indeed going so far as to say: 'It is better that the words of the Law should be burned than that they should be given to a woman'[1]) Christ taught women as He did men. He made no distinction. A group of women followed Him and ministered to Him of their substance. They, with others, formed part of the multitudes to whom He gave instruction. The woman at Samaria's well had a sermon all to herself before the crowd arrived and indeed was instructed in deep spiritual truth with regard, for example, not only to her own deep need but also to the controversy between Mount Gerizim and Mount Zion and to the inner spiritual nature of true worship:

> Jesus saith unto her, Woman, believe me, the hour cometh, when neither in this mountain, nor in Jerusalem, shall ye worship the Father. Ye worship that which ye know not: we worship that which we know: for salvation is from the Jews. But the hour cometh, and now is, when the true worshippers shall worship the Father in spirit and truth: for such doth the Father seek to be his worshippers. God is a Spirit: and they that worship him must worship in spirit and truth (Jn 4:21-24).

Martha, the sister of Mary and Lazarus, received very special instruction regarding the resurrection, prior to the raising of Lazarus from the dead:

> Jesus saith unto her, Thy brother shall rise again. Martha saith unto him, I know that he shall rise again in the resur-

rection at the last day. Jesus said unto her, I am the resurrection, and the life: he that believeth on me, though he die, yet shall he live (Jn 11:23–25).

It is difficult for us to appreciate the revolutionary nature of the actions of Christ in dealing with women in this way. It would not have been so out of keeping in the days of the patriarchs or prophets—but the three hundred years prior to Christ's birth had brought vast changes in Israel. Judaism with all its legalistic rigidity was like a vice upon the minds of men, and women were disgracefully downtrodden.

We should note too that, as He went around the country, Christ allowed women to follow Him from place to place and while we may scarcely notice this in the days of His public ministry, we cannot fail to notice how prominent they became at Calvary and at the tomb. Amongst them were Mary Magdalene, Mary the mother of James and Joses, Salome, Joanna and Susanna. Regarding the crucifixion, we read in Mark 15:40–41:

> And there were also women beholding from afar: among whom were both Mary Magdalene and Mary the mother of James the less and of Joses, and Salome; who, when he was in Galilee, followed him, and ministered unto him; and many other women which came up with him unto Jerusalem,

The fact that Christ allowed women to follow Him receives no particular comment in Scripture itself although it may well have been criticised by many of the Jews. We do read, however, of the surprise of the woman at Samaria's well that Christ should have spoken to her, probably on the twofold ground that she was a Samaritan and a woman. The rabbis would have objected on a third ground—that she was immoral. His disciples certainly registered acute surprise that He should have been found talking to her. Again we should remember the convention of the age that no male Jew should talk to a woman on the street even if she were wife, sister or mother. Against such a background we see Christ risking His reputation on three distinct occasions: the case of the woman in Samaria; the case of the woman taken in adultery (here He showed wondrous grace and tenderness and refused to condemn her); and thirdly the woman described as a sinner who brought the alabaster cruse of ointment, wetting his feet with her tears and drying them with her hair—to the indignation of His host.

Over all, there radiates from Christ an attitude of love and care for all. There is no hint of women being excluded. They were regarded as His friends and indeed were treated with particular grace and kindness.

Thus we say that Christ loved and ministered to women and gladly received their gratitude and worship. He treated them with a dignity and a respect which had been generally lost in the age in which He lived. He instructed them in spiritual truth and in theology and obviously considered them capable of responding. It is no wonder He won their hearts—then, and through all succeeding ages. In His life He restored to women the place they had known in an earlier age. In His death He cancelled the curse that came with the Fall and opened the way to the fulfilment of a destiny beyond the innocency of Eden—as we shall see in a later chapter.

In addition to ministering to Christ of their substance prior to Calvary, the role of the women at Calvary and thereafter is memorable. In love they waited as He died and the scene at the tomb shines with a brightness all its own. It is difficult to get a full and comprehensive picture of the detail of all that happened in these momentous days but, taking the four gospels together, we are left with the picture of a group of women who are less concerned with their own suffering than with His. Being women, they reached right through to the heart of things and were probably untouched by the seeming theological implications of His death. They had known Him and—despite the appearance of things, despite His death—the love, I believe, never faltered and neither, I suggest, did the trust. Mary, His mother, had from earliest days been prepared for such an hour: 'Yea and a sword shall pierce through thine own soul' (Lk 2:35). But what of Mary Magdalene? We read of no such warning in her case. Her story is wonderful:

But Mary was standing without at the tomb weeping: so, as she wept, she stooped and looked into the tomb; And she beholdeth two angels in white sitting, one at the head, and one at the feet, where the body of Jesus had lain. And they say unto her, Woman, why weepest thou? She saith unto them, Because they have taken away my Lord, and I know not where they have laid him. When she had thus said, she turned herself back, and beholdeth Jesus standing, and knew not that it was Jesus. Jesus saith unto her, Woman, why weepest thou? whom seekest thou? She, supposing him to be the gardener, saith unto him, Sir, if thou hast borne him hence, tell me where thou hast laid him, and I will take him away. Jesus saith unto her, Mary. She turneth herself and saith unto him in Hebrew, Rabboni; which is to say, Master. Jesus saith to her, Touch me not; for I am not yet ascended unto the Father: but go unto my brethren and say to them, I ascend unto my Father and your Father, and my God and your God. Mary Magdalene cometh and telleth the disciples, I have seen the Lord; and how that he had said these things unto her (Jn 20:11–18).

Christ had earlier cast seven demons out of Mary and was perhaps the first man who ever treated her with respect and real love. She was forgiven much and she loved much. How could she ever forget the hell from which He had delivered her? The memory of those tormenting demons would always remain but so would the joy of a total deliverance from their power. Men might criticise her Lord but He had done what no one else had ever done—He had set her free and she could not forget. She noted where His dead body was laid and with others prepared spices to embalm Him. The record is fascinating. On the first day of the week she comes early to the tomb and, when alone, looks in and sees two angels, but seems so overcome with the tragedy of not finding Christ that the fact of speaking with the angels seems to have had less significance to her than one might normally have expected. She turns back and mistakes Jesus for the gardener[2] until He speaks her name. Instantly she recognises Him and seeks to touch Him,[3] What a moment of glory! Mary had not only been heart-broken at the death of Christ—she was broken again at the loss of His body. That dead body meant more to her than any other living body in all the world. What a moment of joy! And what an end there is to the story: she, a woman, was the first to see Him on resurrection ground and she was commissioned by Him to be the first herald of His resurrection. Yes, she—a woman —and to whom was she to go? Other women, with no men present? Indeed no—but to men—to His brethren, to witness to the resurrection and coming ascension. A very cornerstone of the gospel is first preached by a woman (and that on the specific command of Christ) and by a woman to men. What a wonderful preaching of doctrine was this and what a wonderful doctrine she preached!

There remains a final section, touched on in the last chapter: the matter of divorce. Briefly, Christ spoke against the current practice of His day when men followed the teaching of Hillel and divorce was easy and granted for trivial reasons. He showed clearly that in God's provision for marriage a man was viewed as leaving father and mother and cleaving to his wife—the two became one flesh. Because of the hardness of the hearts of the Israelites Moses had allowed them to write a bill of divorcement[4]—but then only for serious faults. Christ took the matter out of the sphere of any ambiguous interpretation. Adultery alone was an acceptable ground and He made it clear that divorce was not a provision made by God from the beginning.[5] In short, marriage was before God and seen as life-long and binding.[6] The ground was being prepared for His Church and before long monogamy became the order for elders and deacons and then the custom for all men.

In this area, too, Christ restored dignity and worth to women, and whether particular women in our day ever find Him as Saviour or not, they owe Him a tremendous debt. In the same way He has had such a profound effect on the morals, laws and institutions of the whole Western world, that whether we follow Him or not, we owe Him an almost incalculable debt in natural life. Instead of unconfined greed, cruelty and injustice—so rife where His influence has not spread—there is in our laws and institutions at least an attempt at charity, toleration and justice. We sometimes forget the indirect effect of His influence on the world in attempting to assess the more direct effect of His life and teachings.

Notes

1 From Josephus, *Antiquities*, in Hurley, 'Women in Ministry,' p.126.

2 A real mark of the authenticity of the writing. A prefabricated tale might have indicated instant recognition—but in real life it is not so. I often meet people out of their normal surroundings and sometimes it takes a few moments before recognition is complete. The presence of the living Christ was totally unexpected by Mary.

3 Mary was not allowed to touch Christ because at that point He had not appeared before the Father. Soon afterwards He invited Thomas to handle Him. Presumably by then He had appeared before the Father—perhaps having led 'captivity captive' and taken the saints of Old Testament days to Paradise.

4 While Moses allowed divorce he did not recommend it. In fact he really regulated a related evil practice (remarriage to a first husband after marriage to a second).

5 In Moses' day sexual infidelity was not a matter for divorce but for death and this was the only ground on which Christ allowed divorce. His teaching was far more radical that that of either Hillel or Shammai and occasioned his disciples' shocked surprise. 'If the case of the man is so with his wife, it is not expedient to marry' (Mt 19:10). Christ very clearly showed that with the coming of His Kingdom marriage was to be a permanent life-long contract, which for some of His people was the Divine plan. For others, the way of God's choice was through celibacy. The first of these is sometimes described as creational; the second as re-creational. In our day we are familiar with the teaching. In Christ's day it was radical and far above the teaching of the rabbis. One further point of great significance should be noted in the teaching of Jesus with reference to lust. To avoid sexual temptation the rabbis had encouraged the separation of the sexes. Christ did not take this line. He not only condemned the commission of sin but the lustful attitude which led to it: 'Thou shalt not

commit adultery: but I say unto you, that every one that looketh on a woman to lust after her hath committed adultery with her already in his heart' (Mt 5:27–28). He wanted the heart cleansed. The corollary of this is that women were not segregated and confined. They were free to move in public with men. In a Christian society men were expected to meet temptation and live above it. Christ's attitude on this has profound consequences for the setting of women free.

[6] Some are of the opinion that if Christ allowed divorce for adultery, the innocent party was automatically free to remarry. But Paul's teaching in 1 Corinthians 7:10–16 speaks of the person who deserts her partner not being free to marry another while her husband lives. Thus there appear to be two grounds for divorce: adultery and desertion. Now, if there is not freedom to marry in the case of desertion, it is difficult to see how there can be where adultery is concerned. The whole issue is complex and deserves fuller treatment than I can give it here. I would refer readers to Gordon D. Fee, *The First Epistle to the Corinthians* (Wm. B. Eerdmans Publishing Company, 1987), pp. 267–306, where divorce and remarriage are examined in the context of the First Epistle to the Corinthians.

There is one further issue on which I should perhaps comment. In 1 Corinthians 7:5–6 we read, 'Defraud ye not one the other, except it be by consent for a season, that ye may give yourselves unto prayer, and may be together again, that Satan tempt you not because of your incontinency. But this I say by way of permission, not of commandment.' Husbands and wives were regarded as mutually dependent, and marital duties were to be fulfilled. While there may be difficulty in ascertaining whether Paul's permission related to freedom to take part in sexual activity or to refrain from it temporarily, it is evident that he regarded men and women as having sexual needs which could be properly satisfied within marriage. Thus sex was regarded as meeting more than a procreational need, and by inference it seems that a case for birth control can be based on these verses.

Because of Christ's words regarding eunuchs in Matthew 19:12, some consider celibacy a higher calling than marriage— but surely the truth is that those who fulfil their potential do so by following God's way for them, whether through marriage or celibacy. Let every man and woman find Divine direction; there surely is a plan for every life.

5

Prophesying Daughters

In Acts 1 we read that the eleven apostles 'with one accord continued stedfastly in prayer, with the women, and Mary the mother of Jesus, and with his brethren,' and in Acts 2 Luke continues: 'And when the day of Pentecost was now come, they were all together in one place.' Now when the Book of Acts was written there were no chapter or verse divisions and these two verses establish the fact that there were women in the upper room on the day of Pentecost. This is important in the light of what we next read:

> And suddenly there came from heaven a sound as of the rushing of a mighty wind, and it filled all the house where they were sitting. And there appeared unto them tongues parting asunder, like as of fire; and it sat upon each one of them. And they were all filled with the Holy Spirit, and began to speak with other tongues, as the Spirit gave them utterance (Acts 2:2–4).

Tongues, like as of fire, sat on each of them. They were all filled with the Holy Spirit and they all spoke in tongues as the Spirit gave them utterance. The women were included in all of this. There is no question of their being unaffected or remaining silent on this historic day.

Like the men, they became vocal under Divine power. We should note the emphasis in our reading: a tongue sat on *each* of them; they were *all* filled with the Spirit; they *all* spoke in tongues. There were no exceptions in the upper room.

I have written elsewhere[1] of this occasion in some depth, but perhaps one aspect would bear repeating here since it has relevance to the role of women, particularly in the light of frequent attempts to silence them in public gatherings.

In Acts 1:8, we read:

> But ye shall receive power, when the Holy Ghost is come upon you; and ye shall be my witnesses both in Jerusalem, and in all Judaea and Samaria, and unto the uttermost part of the earth.

'Ye shall be my witnesses.' How does a person normally witness? Surely with the tongue. We come to chapter 2 and read of the outpouring of the Holy Spirit. They already knew Christ as Saviour and Lord. But God was interested in more than their salvation. He was interested in the salvation of others and had ordained that the gospel should be preached by those already redeemed. For this, power was required and power would flow through preaching and preaching in turn would be by human tongue.[2] Thus it is of significance that the symbol of the Holy Spirit in Acts 2 is a tongue like as of fire. We do not read of flaming hands to denote work, or flaming feet to run with the gospel, or flaming shoulders to bear burdens or of a flaming head for thought—nor even a flaming heart to speak of love. Upon everyone there was a flaming tongue. All were to be witnesses. With the tongue witness is given. Every

47

tongue was to be affected. Every woman was involved. Not only then, but for ever afterwards every woman was to be a witness—they were to witness in Judaea, Samaria and, mark it well, to the uttermost parts of the earth. The Baptism gives the initial empowering—on that occasion the tongue is set free—but the experience is not for that hour alone. It is an initial experience. It is an entrance to a whole new life, and the life into which these women entered was one of effective and powerful witness for Jesus Christ. These are inescapable facts.

After the outpouring of the Spirit, Peter addressed the thousands who on hearing the sound had gathered together. By way of explanation he quoted from the prophet Joel:

> And it shall be in the last days, saith God, I will pour forth of my Spirit upon all flesh: And your sons and your daughters shall prophesy, and your young men shall see visions, and your old men shall dream dreams: Yea and on my servants and on my handmaidens in those days will I pour forth of my spirit; and they shall prophesy (Acts 2:17–18).

Now there is much of great interest in this chapter and it is difficult for a writer to leave it alone. However, the particular emphasis of this book is the role and ministry of women and perhaps I had better confine myself to this area.

We note that in the last days the Spirit would be poured on *all* flesh, Women were included. Sons and *daughters* would prophesy. Verse 18 reiterates the fact that in those days the Spirit would be poured on the *handmaidens* and they would prophesy.

These verses are very clearcut and unambiguous. That women were included in the outpouring is evident and the prophetic prediction was fulfilled. Had the prediction, however, spoken only of an inner empowering, it might have been argued that women would receive this and then be used in a silent ministry, such as private prayer. But the matter is left beyond dispute. The women actually spoke in tongues and the prediction envisages 'daughters' and 'handmaidens' prophesying.

Now while prayer may on occasion be silent—prophecy is not. It is a vocal function. It comes by Divine unction and is a means of conveying the mind of God to men. It may, but does not necessarily, include prediction. It is equivalent to tongues combined with interpretation and can include all that interpretation does. 'He that prophesieth,' Paul writes, 'speaketh unto men edification, and comfort, and consolation' (1 Cor 14:3). He further indicates that revelation, knowledge and teaching may be included in interpretation.[3] This is important and will be further considered when we deal with the First Epistle to the Corinthians. Suffice for the moment to establish that prophecy involved public proclamation; that it was a gift from God (and we learn later one of his greatest gifts); that by it came revelation, teaching, knowledge, comfort, consolation and edification; that women were envisaged in Acts 2 as being used in it; and thus, by inference, that women would, under Divine unction, be used in all of these ways. In Acts 21:8-9, we read of the four daughters of Philip the evangelist 'which did prophesy.' Thus it is established that the prediction given by Joel and quoted by Peter was actually fulfilled in the Book of Acts.

There are other matters of particular interest to women in the same book—the story of Dorcas, a woman 'full of good works and alms which she did' whom Peter raised from the dead, and Lydia who opened her house to Paul, but it is when we come to the meeting of Apollos with Priscilla and Aquila that a matter of particular significance for this study emerges. A woman is seen in a very definite role of teacher and not only does she teach, but she teaches a man. We read:

> Now a certain Jew named Apollos, an Alexandrian by race, a learned man, came to Ephesus; and he was mighty in the scriptures. This man had been instructed in the way of the Lord; and being fervent in spirit, he spake and taught carefully the things concerning Jesus, knowing only the baptism of John: and he began to speak boldly in the synagogue. But when Priscilla and Aquila heard him, they took him unto them, and expounded unto him the way of God more carefully (Acts 18:24–26).

Much has been written about Priscilla. We should notice that the instruction given to Apollos was given by Priscilla and Aquila. They were both involved. It may also be significant that Priscilla tends to be first named and was possibly the one who took the lead. There can be no question about the type of instruction given. Doctrine was definitely involved. Apollos knew of the teaching of John relative to Christ and, no doubt, being mighty in the Scriptures, knew many of the Old Testament prophecies which foretold the coming and suffering of Christ. He did not, however, know of the fulfilment of later days. I imagine that such fundamental truths as the atonement, resurrection, ascension and outpouring of the Spirit would be outwith his knowledge and would be amongst the doctrines in which Priscilla and Aquila instructed him 'more carefully'.

Paul had previously met this Jewish couple when he came from Athens to Corinth. With other Jews they had been expelled from Rome by Claudius. They were tent makers and Paul, being of the same trade, stayed and worked with them. When the apostle left for Syria he took Priscilla and Aquila with him. It was some time later that Apollos met the couple in a synagogue in Ephesus.

There are other references to Priscilla in Scripture which are illuminating. She was no ordinary person, no appendage of her husband.

> Salute Prisca and Aquila my fellow-workers in Christ Jesus, who for my life laid down their own necks; unto whom not ionly I give thanks but also all the churches of the Gentiles: And salute the church that is in their house (Rom 16:3–5).

This was a woman, whom Paul seems proud to have described as a 'fellow-worker' and one who risked her life for the gospel, who was appreciated not only by him but by all the gentile churches. This was no mere tea-maker (if I may be anachronistic), sock-darner, flower-arranger or house-minder. This, one instinctively feels, was a woman of full-blooded action. I really cannot believe that her lips were sealed or her drive for God inhibited by any question of her sex.

Surely there comes from the Book of Acts a sense that the winds of liberation are blowing. Thank God! For me, at least, as we move further into Romans, 1 Corinthians and Galatians, the winds become a veritable gale.

Do lift the heavy anchors of prejudice and tradition and set your sails to catch the wind of God.

Notes

[1] See Hugh B. Black *Reflections on the Baptism in the Holy Spirit* (New Dawn Books, 1987), chap.5.
[2] We should remember the words of Christ: 'All authority (or power) hath been given unto me in heaven and on earth. Go

ye therefore, and make disciples of all the nations.' (Mt 28:18). This envisages an endless supply of Divine power. 'But ye shall receive power, when the Holy Ghost is come upon you' (Acts 1:8). The channels through which the power was to flow were human. The Gospel, Paul said, 'is the power of God unto salvation to everyone that believeth' (Rom 1:16).

Around us there is almost an infinite sea of human need; above us an infinite sea of Divine power. How is the power to meet the need? Surely it is to flow through human channels.

I am reminded of the oft-told story of Christ speaking to an archangel after His return to glory. On being asked about His plans for the future of the kingdom He speaks of the work He has left in the hands of men. 'What,' said the archangel, 'are you trusting them again?' 'Yes,' He said, 'I am trusting them again!' Wonderful, is it not? He passed angels by when He laid hold on the seed of Abraham and shared our humanity. Now He does not commit the preaching of the gospel to angels but to men. Finally, He will one day take redeemed men to be His eternal bride. Not only will we judge angels, but we will be heirs of God and joint heirs with Christ. Let us in our present experience rejoice in partaking of His power and being used in His service to His glory.

3 When Paul's argument for the necessity of tongues being interpreted is closely followed, it becomes obvious from 1 Corinthians 14:6 that the things he lists there may all be contained in interpretation. This is not immediately apparent, but on examination becomes inescapable.

6

Fellow Labourers with Paul

In the Book of Acts we met Priscilla and Aquila and their links with Paul took us into the epistle to the Romans, but before moving on, there are one or two other matters to consider.

In Romans 16:1–12 we read of Phoebe and Junia(s) and a number of other women who 'laboured' in the Lord. What the labour was is not precisely defined—but there is no faintest indication that it was at all menial. The women were obviously viewed by Paul as fellow workers. Prisca (short for Priscilla) is so defined and Mary, Tryphaena, Tryphosa and Persis all laboured with Paul. Now Paul's work was missionary work and the women are seen here as fully involved.[1]

The cases of Phoebe and Junia call for special comment.

In 1 Timothy 3 the qualifications for elders and deacons are listed and in the very midst of the discussion on deacons a third group is introduced: '*Women* in like manner must be grave, not slanderers, temperate, faithful in all things' (verse 11).

Of the deacons we read: 'Deacons in like manner must be grave, not double-tongued, not given to much wine, not greedy of filthy lucre' (verse 8). The question arises:

who were these women? Various suggestions have been made but there seems to be a fair consensus amongst scholars that they were, in fact, women deacons. The word Paul uses—*gynaikes*—may mean either women or wives, but the construction of the passage indicates a class parallel to the elders and deacons, rather than wives of the latter. In addition, the qualifications given for the women parallel those for the male deacons.[2] In my view there were recognised women deacons in the New Testament and Phoebe was one of them.

> I commend unto you Phoebe our sister, who is a servant of the church that is at Cenchreae: that ye receive her in the Lord, worthily of the saints, and that ye assist her in whatsoever matter she may have need of you: for she herself also hath been a succourer of many, and of mine own self (Rom 16:1–2).

The case of Junia raises quite a different issue. 'Salute Andronicus and Junia(s), my kinsmen, and my fellow-prisoners, who are of note among the apostles, who also have been in Christ before me' (Rom 16:7). There has been much debate about the gender of Junia(s). The form of the name at least admits the possibility that a woman is referred to. There is not, however, complete agreement amongst scholars on the point.

It should be noted too that many more than the original twelve are referred to as apostles in the New Testament. That does not mean that later apostles were all on a par with the original group—although Paul could describe himself as being 'not a whit behind the very chiefest apostles.' Indeed we may not assume that later apostles would be greater or less great than those first called. They would, however, be in a different category.

In 1 Corinthians, chapters 7 and 11 in particular first claim our attention. In 7:16 we read: 'For how knowest thou, O wife, whether thou shalt save thy husband?'

In practical terms what does this really mean? The school of thought which forbids women ever to teach men must find the same kind of difficulty here as arises with the case of Priscilla and other women who 'laboured' with Paul in the gospel on what was then the mission field. It is unrealistic to suppose that the mouths of the women were closed to communicating anything of the things of God. Was a saved woman to refuse to tell her husband how to find Christ? If she had sons might she not instruct them either? Was her teaching to be confined solely to women or girls? At home, or on missionary service was she to speak only to her own sex?

In this verse she is seen as saving her husband. It is good to remind ourselves of what we noticed earlier regarding witnessing in Acts 1 and 2. Witness was by the tongue and the tongue was set on fire by God. Women were numbered with the witnesses and any idea of their not telling the good news to their own husbands is surely ludicrous. In the light of these verses and of the fact that Psalm 68:11 says, 'The women that publish the tidings are a great host,' some leaders are prepared to allow women to preach while refusing to allow them to teach. Now while it is true that there is a shade of difference between preaching and teaching, the second is often a function of the first. If, for example, a woman preaches the gospel to a man she is in reality *teaching* the doctrine of salvation. In my view it has to be accepted that women taught in New Testament days and that they taught men. This theme recurs in 1 Corinthians 14. The difficulty regarding teaching (which is very real in the minds of many honest Christians) will be further investigated when we come to 1 Timothy 2:11–13. Almost the whole difficulty rises from this passage.

In 1 Corinthians 11:3–15, we read:

> But I would have you know, that the head of every man is Christ; and the head of the woman is the man; and the head of Christ is God. Every man praying or prophesying, having his head covered, dishonoureth his head. But every woman praying or prophesying with her head unveiled dishonoureth her head: for it is one and the same thing as if she were shaven. For if a woman is not veiled, let her also be shorn: but if it is a shame to a woman to be shorn or shaven, let her be veiled. For a man indeed ought not to have his head veiled, forasmuch as he is the image and glory of God; but the woman is the glory of the man. For the man is not of the woman; but the woman of the man: for neither was the man created for the woman; but the woman for the man: for this cause ought the woman to have a sign of authority on her head, because of the angels. Howbeit neither is the woman without the man, nor the man without the woman, in the Lord. For as the woman is of the man, so is the man also by the woman; but all things are of God. Judge ye in yourselves: is it seemly that a woman pray unto God unveiled? Doth not even nature itself teach you, that, if a man have long hair, it is a dishonour to him? But if a woman have long hair it is a glory to her: for her hair is given her for a covering.

Women, as we noted earlier, had two very distinct roles. Indeed they almost lived in two different worlds. In the home sphere, the Bible consistently teaches that they are under male authority. In the spiritual sphere, they are independent of man and answerable to God only. This passage is particularly interesting in these connections. As the woman came into the public assembly—the place **where God was worshipped in a particular way**—she was more or less to leave her femininity behind her. As a woman she had been created for the man. In the human relationship she was made a helpmeet for him. She was made in his image and reflected his glory.[3] In the outside world, marks of her femininity were becoming to her— but when she appeared as a worshipper of God in a public gathering she did not appear as a woman—as distinct from man—but as a redeemed person with an identity of her own and a direct relationship with God quite independent of man. For this reason the sign of her femininity was to be removed. With her head uncovered or shaven her female position was evident. When her hair was covered or veiled her femininity was closed off. The covering was a sign of authority. (In my view this indicated that she was not available.) We should remember she was taking part in church, in deeply spiritual functions—she was moving in a spiritual realm, a realm in which there could be angelic activity and presence. We should also remember that while she was in the image of man and reflected his glory, he had been created in the image of God and reflected His Glory. The beauty of her appearance therefore might well have had attraction for angels.[4] The context seems to suggest such a possibility. The veiling of the hair would be a clear indication to them that she was, as a woman, reserved for man and under his authority. By having the covering, her sexuality was cut off and she was free to move in the spiritual world not as a woman as distinct from man, but as an individual in exactly the same way as a man.

We should always remember that the division of the sexes is related to natural and not to spiritual life.

As indicated in the first chapter of this book, the woman required to have her head covered for another and quite different reason. Man, being in God's image and reflecting His glory, was not allowed to cover his head in God's presence since that would amount to veiling God's glory—but since woman, having been made in the man's image, reflected man's glory she had to cover that glory in His presence. No glory save His own was to be reflected there.

It should be noted that two different Greek words are translated 'covering' (or 'covered') in this passage in the Authorised Version of the Bible and this has caused confusion to many readers. The hair is seen as a covering and this covering has itself to be covered. The Revised Version distinguishes between the two by using 'veiling' for the second and this clarifies the matter.[5]

Now the main point in examining this passage lies not so much in the foregoing, interesting as it is, but in the fact that the woman is seen praying or prophesying in public and doing so in a gathering in which men are present. I have indicated earlier that while prayer can be silent (although I do not think for one moment that it was in this case) prophecy cannot. The latter involves outward, vocal expression. In it, the whole company, including the men, are addressed. It may include comfort, edification, consolation, rebuke, revelation, exhortation, teaching and this is apparent from what Paul indicates in chapter 14 of this same letter to the Corinthians. Thus women are envisaged as teaching men—and not only so, but the form of teaching is one of the very highest: it is by the direct and full inspiration of the Holy Spirit. It is not by a mere function of the human spirit. It is vital to remember this point as we move into chapter 14 and consider verses 34–36 which have caused so much difficulty to so many people through the years.

Notes

[1] In Philippians 4:2, we read of Euodia and Syntyche who were also engaged with Paul in missionary work. They are described as women who 'laboured with me in the gospel.'

[2] Hurley argues the case for women deacons very persuasively in a brief passage in 'Women in Ministry' in The Role of Women, pp.137–139. He goes into greater detail in Man and Woman in Biblical Perspective, pp.122–124.

[3] I would draw attention to the fact that man and woman are spoken of in Genesis as being in the image of God, and that while Paul does not explicitly state that woman was in man's image, he does say that she reflected man's glory. Since woman was taken out of man and in a peculiar sense was part of man, may she not reasonably be regarded as being in his image? Various commentators do point out that Paul did not explicitly state that woman was in man's image.

[4] Consideration of Genesis 6:2–5 may be of interest in this connection:

. . . the sons of God saw the daughters of men that they were fair; and they took them wives of all that they chose . . . and also after that, when the sons of God came in unto the daughters of men, and they bear children to them . . . the Lord saw that the wickedness of man was great in the earth, and that every imagination of the thoughts of his heart was only evil continually.

[5] Hurley holds a very different view of this passage. He argues that a woman's hair properly coiffured constituted her covering and that this did not require to be veiled. He views the woman as second to man but above the angels. Out of respect to man and angels she should show her femininity—not conceal it. This he considers is done by having her hair properly arranged. He alludes to this as the 'out of respect for the angels' theory as distinct from the 'aroused angels' theory which I have suggested. For a fuller account of Hurley's views see Man and Woman in Biblical Perspective, pp.162–184.

For students interested in a detailed exegesis of 1 Corinthians 11:3–15, I recommend Gordon D. Fee's *The First Epistle to the Corinthians*, pp. 512–524. While he takes the view that Paul intended women's hair to be covered, Fee would for cultural reasons, however, approve of women dispensing with hats in our day.

The New International Version (NIV) should also be consulted. It suggests the possibility that the woman's long hair was in fact the covering that Paul demanded. On this view hats or veils would not be obligatory.

7

Silent or Speaking?

Let the women keep silence in the churches; for it is not permitted unto them to speak; but let them be in subjection, as also saith the law. And if they would learn anything, let them ask their own husbands at home: for it is shameful for a woman to speak in the church. What? was it from you that the word of God went forth? or came it unto you alone? (1 Cor 14:34–36).

To find out the meaning of these verses, there are five views which should be considered.

First it should be noted that they do not appear uniformly in this position in all the early manuscripts. They are sometimes included elsewhere in 1 Corinthians though never omitted altogether. This has caused some scholars to take the view that they were not in the original epistle at all, but were inserted later by a scribe as a marginal note, the note in due time becoming incorporated in the text.[1] It is thought that they may be based on 1 Timothy 2, the authenticity of which is not in doubt. The position of the verses in chapter 14 is certainly strange. They come right in the middle of a discussion of spiritual gifts and seem in no way related to these. This lends weight to the argument that they may be a later addition. It is not everyone, however, who will be happy to accept this kind of interpretation and we must look at the verses in a straightforward way.

Secondly we should note that 1 Corinthians 14:34–35 seems to be closely associated with the oral law and it may be that some in Corinth were teaching this.[2] Paul may be viewed as questioning this critically in verse 36. 'What?' he said, 'was it from you that the word of God went forth? or came it unto you alone?' In other words—'Who do you think you are to bring these ideas into the Church? [He might indeed have gone on to say—'I have told you earlier in this letter how women are to be dressed when they prophesy in church. Who are you to bring in past customs of Jews to a gentile gathering and command women to be silent?'] The word of God neither went out from you nor came it to you alone. Do not usurp a position which is not yours.'

On the other hand, and to be fair in commenting, one might view verses 34 and 35 as expressing the writer's views and verse 36 as expressing his indignation that they were not being obeyed. However, our knowledge of Paul's clear teaching elsewhere, e.g., 1 Corinthians 11, rules this interpretation out of court.

In the third place, if we take the passage to mean literally what a superficial reading might convey, we are left to ponder the following points: Women are to be totally silent—totally mute—in the church. They are not to be permitted to speak at all. Indeed it would be shameful for them to do so. If there is anything they require to know they should ask their own husbands about the matter at home. They are to be in subjection.

Now immediately problems arise with this interpretation. If a woman is to be totally silent in church, she cannot possibly prophesy or speak in tongues or pray publicly, and she is envisaged as doing all of these things with scriptural warrant, as we have already seen. Thus, whatever the 'speaking' refers to here it cannot refer to her exercising any of these functions. In my view there is really a very simple explanation of the matter as will appear shortly but, before leaving our consideration of this particular interpretation of the passage, it is worth observing that even the most rigid opponents of women ministry do not apply it literally in practice. In their gatherings women are allowed to sing—thereby breaking silence. Realising that women are given permission to pray, as in 1 Corinthians 11:5, they try to evade the difficulty of allowing her to do this by viewing her as fulfilling her prayer role by being identified with the prayers of the men—her saying of the Amen including her in that. But this in no way helps the case. *Saying the Amen*—precisely—breaking silence. In view of other direct Scriptures and the general tenor of the New Testament this view must also be ruled totally out of court.

Recently I have come on a fourth view which seems to be having a vogue at present but which again I find unsatisfactory. It is argued that immediately prior to the verses related to women, Paul had been giving instructions about prophecy and how it was to be discerned. There was to be no confusion in the church. If a revelation was given to one prophet when another was speaking, the latter was to keep silence while the other took over. They were not to speak together. Since there were no verse divisions in the original writing the idea of silence in verse 30 might seem to lead on naturally to silence in verse 34 in its application to women. In the earlier part, prophecy was to be discerned and now it is suggested that women were not to take part in the judging of prophecy or in discussing it or indeed in asking any questions about it at all. This view associates the instructions about women being silent directly with the discerning or judging of prophecy and maintains that women are to have no part in this.[3] Exponents of the view consider that the prohibition applies to a particular circumstance and does not preclude women from other recognised vocal activities.

I find this unsatisfactory on three counts. First I feel it strains the text and smacks of special pleading. The interjection of the subject of the activity of women is, as we have noted earlier, distinctly strange in the context where it appears—but that does not justify trying to make things fit and manufacturing connections where none may exist.

Secondly, surely it was the prophets who were to judge prophecy and just as surely women were prophets and so qualified to judge. Nor can it be argued that this was a governmental matter in which only men had a role — it was a distinctly spiritual matter and one in which women were already clearly and very properly involved.

Finally, if the silence of women is to be linked to the silence of the prophet, the linking would surely deal with the giving of prophecy and not with its discernment. Thus if we adopt this way of looking at the two passages it would be more natural to view Paul as forbidding women to prophesy. And this, from earlier evidence, is manifestly incorrect. Again the case must be abandoned.

The fifth, and to my mind the only satisfactory interpretation of 1 Corinthians 14:34–36, is really very simple and straightforward. It was the custom in these days for men and women to sit at different sides of the synagogue[4] and there was not generally the reverence in services which we associate with Christian worship.

Questions were shouted by the women to their husbands while services were in progress and indeed this practice seems still to be followed in at least some synagogues right into our own day. Paul had no intention of having this behaviour in the young churches which he founded and he legislated against it. The prohibition on the women was in no way related to their spiritual worship but to natural conduct unbecoming in a worshipping situation. There are two types of silence—one where chattering or ordinary non-spiritual talk is concerned; the other where spiritual worship is envisaged. In the first case silence in enjoined; in the second it is totally unacceptable. Perhaps a very simple illustration will help make this clearer. I was once a school teacher and from time to time I could come into a class which was making an undue noise and firmly say, 'Be quiet there—not another word out of you!' Within a few moments I could lift up a history book and perhaps say, 'Jean, where did we stop last week?' Jean shakes her head and puts her hand across her lips and does not answer. I say, 'Jean, I am speaking to you. Where did we stop last week?' Finally she retorts, 'You said I was to be quiet and not say another word. I am just doing what you told me.' Explosion of dominie! The position is perfectly obvious. Jean was to be totally silent where one form of behaviour was concerned; she was to be vocal when it came to answering a question related to the work of the class.

I understand that Jewish believers never have any difficulty in understanding this passage. It poses no problems and in no way inhibits their women.

There are two passages in the Bible which are mainly used against women ministry. This is the first of these and in my view it presents no real difficulty. The second comes from the first letter of Paul to Timothy nd it will be examined in due course.

Before leaving 1 Corinthians 14, however, one or two points should be emphasised. Since women prophesied they were engaged not only in an exhortative function but in a function which could contain reproof and judgment (see verse 24). That teaching was included in interpretation has already been noticed. Verse 6 specifically mentions it. Thus women are seen teaching in church and in circumstances where men are present.

In verse 26 we read:

> When ye come together, each one hath a psalm, hath a teaching, hath a revelation, hath a tongue, hath an interpretation. Let all things be done unto edifying.

Note the words 'each one'—this included women and note what they are envisaged as doing: singing (hath a psalm), teaching, prophesying (hath a revelation), speaking in tongues, interpreting.

Surely woman's role was a very full and active role indeed.

Notes

[1] Fee argues from both external and internal evidence that verses 34–36 form no part of the original letter to the Corinthians. He presents his view very persuasively, and his exegesis of the portion is particularly interesting. He is certainly in no doubt that these verses should not prevent women from speaking in church. I recommend his work to all serious students.

[2] Fee comments: 'Because of the very Jewish nature of this passage, others have argued that it does not represent Paul's point of view at all, but rather is a quotation or restatement

of the view of some Corinthians who were were imposing it on the community. Usually this is associated with the "Cephas party" of 1:12. Vv. 36–38 are then viewed as Paul's own response to this imposition of "the Law" on the church.' *First Epistle to the Corinthians*, pp. 704–705.

[3] Hurley takes the view that the silence of women in these verses relates to the judging of prophecy only. Otherwise they were free to take part vocally in church services. He considers the verses to be in their proper setting. While I have a very high regard for Hurley's scholarship, I find him quite unconvincing in his interpretation of this passage. See *Man and Woman in Biblical Perspective*, pp. 185–194.

[4] Commenting on procedure in certain synagogues, Professor Barclay indicates that women 'were shut apart in a section of the Synagogue, or in a gallery, where they could not be seen.' *The Daily Study Bible: The Letters to Timothy, Titus and Philemon* (The Saint Andrew Press, 2nd ed., 1960), p. 76.

8

No Sex in Soul

In this chapter we look at Galatians 3:27–28 and Colossians 3:9–11.

> For as many of you as were baptized into Christ did put on Christ. There can be neither Jew nor Greek, there can be neither bond nor free, there can be no male and female: for ye all are one man in Christ Jesus.

> Lie not one to another; seeing that ye have put off the old man with his doings, and have put on the new man, which is being renewed unto knowledge after the image of him that created him: where there cannot be Greek and Jew, circumcision and uncircumcision, barbarian, Scythian, bondman, freeman: but Christ is all, and in all.

I do not want to dull the clarity of this chapter with a multiplicity of words. In these passages we look at a fundamental truth on which many a godly woman has taken her stand:

> There can be neither Jew nor Greek, there can be neither bond nor free, there can be no male and female: for ye are all one man in Christ Jesus.

Let me say it again: 'there can be no male and female.'

Surely the walls of partition are broken down and Christ is all in all.

This, in my view, is one of the two clearest evidences of the equality of women found in the New Testament. She is still a woman, is still distinguished from man by her sex, is still subject to him in her natural life—but as a spiritual being she is totally free and fully equal.

When the 'new man' (who is after the image of God) has been put on, to use Paul's picturesque language, there can no longer be Greek and Jew, circumcision and uncircumcision, Scythian, bondman, freeman. Christ is all and in all. Liberated souls, both men and women, have broken free of their earthly bondages. Race division, slavery, sex division—while still remaining in their natural lives—are abolished as they move into the dimension which is theirs in Christ.

A lovely consistency runs through Bible teaching, and principles which we have noticed right from Eden continue to apply. The woman has her continuing role in relation to man. She has a totally independent role in relationship to God. As she moves in the second realm she is complete in Christ—not complete in a man and then, through the man, complete in Christ. It is a separate completeness. It must surely follow that in this realm all spiritual functions which are open to him must be open to her—otherwise the words 'there is no male and female' could not be true. What does this really mean? And how widely embracing is it? To my mind the horizons are as wide, and the opportunities as unlimited, for the woman as for the man. All spiritual functions open to him are open to her. We have seen that she prophesied and in so doing was used in a vocal function at the highest level. In this activity, teaching was included. We have read of her as labouring with

Paul in the gospel. This shows her in a missionary role in a full-blooded way. She may have been an apostle as in the case of Junia. That Pheobe was a deaconess seems irrefutable. The women of 1 Timothy 5:2[1] were elders. The Greek word used to denote them is *presbyteras*, and this is exactly the same word (with a feminine ending) as is used for the office of elder in this and other contexts with reference to men. Where do we stop? There is no stopping point! When we rid our minds of the prejudices of the ages we grasp the underlying spiritual truth of the total freedom of women in the realm of the Spirit, and then the ministry of women like Amy Carmichael, the Maréchale, and Kathryn Kuhlman becomes understandable. Prejudices, however, can run very deep. They get right into the warp and woof of our thinking and it sometimes takes God Himself to set us free.

That God has used women mightily in our own day is undeniable. General Booth is quoted as saying: 'My best men are women'. The Maréchale, his eldest daughter, was used to bring many thousands to Christ. She was an anointed pioneer and founder of churches. She exercised an apostolic ministry. Amy Carmichael wonderfully led a work of God in Dohnavur. Kathryn Kuhlman was used in a remarkable way and, in her particular ministry, seems to have been not one whit behind any man through all the centuries since Paul's own day. Dare I tell the story again?[2] On the one occasion when I was privileged to hear her I had to wait in a very long queue before being admitted to the vast auditorium where she was preaching. In the crowd around me there was a man (whom I took to be a minister) who was carefully explaining to his friends that it was not God's will to use women but because He could not find a suitable man in America He had chosen

Kathryn Kuhlman, in the same way as He had chosen
Deborah in Old Testament times. In that case too it was
not that He wanted Deborah but He simply took her
because there was no man available. Well! Well! This
view does not say much for either the men of America
in our day or the men of Israel in Deborah's day.

Through the years, many Christians who have been
intellectually convinced that the Bible speaks against
women ministry have had their shocks as it has become
evident that God has greatly anointed and greatly used
some particular woman. It has seemed to go right against
the rules. Often the woman used has been deeply criticised—as was the Maréchale on the occasion when she
made the famous retort, 'But there is no sex in soul.'
Again and again the critic has gone away, however, with
a fearful problem, and it is a problem to which all honest
people must find an answer. God makes no mistakes. A
woman is chosen, anointed and used; her labours and
ministry are fruitful—sometimes abundantly fruitful.
Now who anoints her? What power works through her?
Manifestly, God—and the power is God's! 'By their
fruits ye shall know them.' God is God and His actions
are perfect. *He* does it and He does it again and again
and, may I say it—were it not for our prejudices, and
the prejudices of women themselves, I believe He would
do it much more widely. Yes, although there are perhaps
six women on the mission field for every man, women are
still deeply inhibited. Many never consider themselves
eligible for full-scale action for God. They never open
themselves to it. Speaking reverently, they tie the hands
of God. As we move into the last days this must change.
The women who 'publish the tidings' must become 'a
great host.' Sisters, arise—you have nothing to lose but
your bonds.

71

Again let me emphasise it—it is God who speaks through the prophetess. It is the Holy Spirit Who has so manifestly anointed women. Who can gainsay it? 'Ah,' you say, 'but the Bible says. . . .' My friend, God never opposes His own Word. He is forever constant. What He forbids, He forbids. What He commands, He commands. He never moves against Himself—else would His kingdom be divided. Be careful therefore. Is it not just possible that you have mistakenly interpreted what the Bible says? The Holy Spirit, you know, would lead you into all truth. I take the view that the Bible wholly supports women ministry and is in no single case inconsistent. And ever in the background there lies the knowledge that God Himself moves women to preach and teach and blesses their ministry. This is inescapable and unanswerable. Would to God that all our Christian women, who far outnumber our men, would mobilise for battle. Surely this is the hour!

Notes

[1] 'Rebuke not an elder, but exhort him as a father . . . the elder women as mothers' (1 Tim 5:1–2).

[2] More fully related in *Reflections on the Baptism in the Holy Spirit*, pp. 23–24.

9

Usurpers of Authority

Although 1 Timothy 2:11–15 is the most difficult scripture in relation to our subject, it was from this very passage that I had illumination which has greatly affected my outlook and which forms, in my opinion, the second of the two strongest arguments for the equality of women with men.

> Let a woman learn in quietness with all subjection. But I permit not a woman to teach, nor to have dominion over a man, but to be in quietness. For Adam was first formed, then Eve; and Adam was not beguiled,[1] but the woman being beguiled hath fallen into transgression: but she shall be saved through the childbearing,[2] if they continue in faith and love and sanctification with sobriety (1 Tim 2:11–15).

We must first consider what 'quietness' and 'subjection' meant and secondly what the nature of 'teaching' was and what kind of 'dominion' was referred to.

Consistently throughout this work it has been argued that women have had two distinct roles: in relationship to men in the domestic sphere and in relationship to God. In the first she has been seen as subject; in the second the subjection is to God only. In the first man has dominion; in the second God alone is to exercise control. In the first man has a role; in the second he has no place. Thus in the home sphere no problem of definition arises. The man is the head and carries responsibility as such. Where worship and the service of God are concerned woman is free of man's headship and knows only God's. The vital question now arises—do these views fully accord with Paul's instructions to Timothy contained in the verses before us?

Perhaps it is wise to consider first the way in which commentators who oppose women ministry view the passage. In the extreme camp are those who define women's role as one in which they attend to home matters in subjection to their husbands. They pray in private and may instruct other women if no men are present. In the church sphere they may neither preach nor teach nor pray. They may take no part in the government of the church.

Now it is quite obvious from Scriptures which we have already considered that this extreme view is quite untenable. Women undoubtedly did pray and prophesy in church as 1 Corinthians 11 clearly reveals. Thus I feel it will be more fruitful to concentrate on the more difficult argument that moderate exponents of the opposition advance than to spend time on the extreme view.

The moderate school generally recognises that women may be used in the inspirational field. They may be used in any or all of the gifts of the Spirit. They may pray and prophesy publicly—but the line is drawn, at least by some, at preaching and teaching. They may exercise no governmental role.

It has to be recognised that a great number of very honest students of the Bible who have no anti-woman bias, hold this view. They reverence the Word of God and are most anxious to obey it. They genuinely feel that, apart from anything else, the Timothy Scripture makes the conclusion they have reached inescapable where teaching is concerned. On the matter of preaching there is sometimes a less rigid line and testifying is frequently allowed.

Now this to me seems inconsistent. A woman is seen prophesying—in which gift she is used by God in a very direct way to give fully inspired utterance which, as we have already seen, may contain teaching and rebuke. Its purpose is to edify the whole church, including the men. She is seen in one of the highest functions of vocal utterance. That she may prophesy is beyond doubt. Preaching and teaching, on the other hand, are often viewed (not quite accurately, I suggest) as less inspirational and more humanly-based activities. In these she is to take no part. But surely, if these activities are less inspirational, they are lower activities than prophesying. If the woman is free to take part in the greater ministry who can exclude her from the lesser? It does not make sense. To put it in blunt terms: a woman may in prophecy give glorious teaching direct from God Himself; she may not, however, according to this school, rise in the assembly and explain a doctrine such as baptism in water or the atonement, which are already outlined in Scripture. God trusts her at the higher level; man does not trust her at the lower. God is prepared to give revelation of new things (not inconsistent with things already revealed—but new) with particular relevance to new circumstances. She is a vehicle for His living word. Is this a lower activity than that engaged in by a man who applies his fallen intelligence to instructing in doctrine? I think not.

I would note, in passing, that in my view *all* preaching and teaching *should* be inspired. I do not think God expects less. If we are truly dead to self as we ought to be, and are filled with the Holy Spirit, we should surely be His mouthpieces. Many years ago I noticed that Charles G. Finney taught that the gospel, for example, ought never to be preached other than in the power of the Spirit. He maintained that otherwise it could have a hardening and harmful effect. I agree. We pitch our sights too low. If we expect the mediocre we will get the mediocre. If we look to move only under Divine power surely He will be with us. We must seek to attain this position.

We have reached the point in the argument where I have maintained that prophecy is greater than preaching and teaching, at least as the latter are generally defined by the school whose view of women ministry I am opposing. To allow women to prophesy and forbid to teach seems totally unreasonable and untenable.

What then can the verses mean? Paul undoubtedly gave the instruction.[3] Let us first note that the epistle to Timothy is a letter to an individual and not to a church.[4] Why then are these instructions so often assumed to apply to conduct in a church gathering? We face the question: Do the verses relate to the woman in the domestic sphere, or do they apply to her activity in the world of worship and the service of God?

If we view the instruction as applying to church activity we are immediately in trouble. She is to learn in quietness. She is not to teach. Now in our study of 1 Corinthians 14 it clearly emerged that while there was one way in which she was to be quiet or silent[5] there was another in which she was to be active and vocal. She was to pray and as a prophetess she was engaged in teaching and in teaching men. In Acts 18 Priscilla, a woman, instructed Apollos in the way of the Lord. Paul freely acknowledged the help which women gave him in the gospel. They were co-workers. He recognised them as fellow labourers and the word suggests that he viewed them as having much more than a servile role. We cannot have it both ways—the women cannot observe silence and be vocal at the same time; they cannot be forbidden to teach and be exhorted to prophesy at one and the same time. Surely we are involved in impossible contradiction with this view.

On the other hand, if we apply the verses to the woman in the home sphere we suddenly realise that these instructions conform exactly with what Paul has taught elsewhere, for example in 1 Corinthians 11, and with what the Bible consistently teaches from the hour when Eve was excluded from Eden and put under the rule of Adam—'thy desire shall be to thy husband, and he shall rule over thee'. *She* is not in the dominant role. The *man* is. In this field she is in the learning role and he in the instructing role. She is to accept this quietly. Now we come to the words, 'I permit not a woman to teach, nor to have dominion over a man.' What does the word 'teach' mean? First let it be acknowledged that it is translated from a Greek word which *could* be and *was* at times applied to instruction in doctrine—but it had, and indeed still has, a wider meaning.[6] A clue to the wider meaning lies in the phrase 'have dominion'. The Authorised Version makes this even clearer. There it reads 'usurp authority'. In our use of language the words 'or' and 'nor' are used conjunctively or disjunctively. In other words, they join things that are similar or separate things that are different. For example, I might say to a boy, 'You have a choice. You can have either a bicycle or a computer for your Christmas present.' Here the 'or' separates things that are different—the bicycle and the computer. I might, on the other hand, be displeased with the boy and say, 'I will not allow you to bully or ill-treat your sister.' Here the 'or' joins words which have similar meanings—bully, ill-treat. The word ill-treat explains the word bully or at least gives a flavour of the meaning. When we apply this to the statement, 'I permit not a woman to teach, nor to usurp authority over the man,' and view the 'nor' as conjunctive we find that the words 'usurp authority' or 'have dominion' explain what teaching means in this context. As a school teacher I could say to an unruly class, as I exerted authority over them: 'I'll teach you never to disobey me again.' That is one meaning of 'teach'. There is another. I could say: 'We are nearing examination time and I still have to teach the First World War.' That is quite a different meaning of 'teach'.

Thus, when we apply the words to the domestic sphere all is consistent. For a woman to teach her husband, in the sense of taking the leading and dominating role, is forbidden. This taking of authority would involve usurpation and the taking of something that was not hers.[7] It would involve her in coming out of her Divinely appointed role and taking on herself the role God had ordained for the man. When we interpret the passage in this way there is no contradiction of any other teaching of Scripture. Everything falls into place. To view the teaching, on the other hand, as applying to spiritual instruction raises insuperable difficulties.

In prophecy, teaching, and so on, it is the Holy Spirit Who is speaking through the woman. The woman does not usurp authority. You are in a higher realm where no human has authority at all—only God. Therefore, this Scripture may be understood as applying to the natural sphere where man is in authority.

Notes

1 Some have suggested that the word translated 'beguiled' carries overtones of sexual seduction, and that as 'an angel of light' Satan may have had dealings with Eve. I find the theory both repulsive and ill-founded.

2 This in no way suggests that a woman is saved through having a family or that she ought to marry. Nor to my mind does it mean that she is saved in the sense of being saved from usurping man's role by the demands of attending to a family, or through finding 'her natural vocation in a life of domesticity in subordination to her husband,' as some have suggested. See A. T. Hanson, *The Pastoral Epistles* (Wm. B. Eerdmans Publishing Company, 1982), p. 74.

Another view which will be of interest to readers is that women are saved from judgment or from death in childbirth (*ibid.*) An interpretation suggested by Hurley reads: 'Eve will be saved from the curse through the birth of the promised child, Jesus, and other women who exhibit obedient faith will similarly be saved' (*Man and Woman in Biblical Perspective*, p. 222). See also Barclay, who suggests that 'women will find life and salvation . . . in motherhood, which is their crown' (*The Letters to Timothy, Titus and Philemon*, p. 79).

3 There has, of course, been debate amongst scholars about the authorship of the Pastoral Epistles and the degree to which Paul may have been involved in them. This is not, however, of particular relevance to our present study. The canonical nature of the books is not in doubt.

4 It is recognised, of course, that the letter does give guidance as to 'how men ought to behave themselves in the house of God' (1 Tim 3:15). It is not, however, stated that the views under consideration refer particularly to a church setting. Indeed, verse 8 of chapter 2 speaks of men praying in *every* place, lifting up holy hands. Verse 9 speaks of women's dress and to my mind very obviously has a general application.

I have searched carefully and unsuccessfully for concrete evidence that a church gathering is envisaged in verses 11-

15. It obviously *may* have been, but we are not told that it *was*. Some commentators argue in favour, from 1 Corinthians 7:16, where a wife is seen as saving her husband. The reasoning seems to be as follows. At home the woman is instructing the husband in the way of salvation, and since this in their view clashes with the Timothy verses, these, they conclude, must refer to a church setting. This of course is not the only possible solution. Another, and to my mind much better, is that teaching here refers to usurping authority in the home sphere.

5 The Greek word for 'silence' in 1 Corinthians 14:34 comes from the verb *sigaō*. The word translated 'quietness' in 1 Timothy 2:11, 12 is *hēsychia*. This carried the thought of desistance from bustle.

6 The word 'teach' is translated from *didaskō* and means 'teach' but with a very broad or general application. It is quite different from the 'apt to teach' of 1 Timothy 3:2 where bishops are referred to. In the second case the word is *didaktikos*, which carries the thought of 'instructive' in the 'didactic' sense. There are actually several words in the New Testament translated 'teach,' but that used in 1 Timothy 2:12 is one in particular which does not narrow the meaning to doctrine. For instance, the same word is used in 1 Corinthians 11:14, 'Doth not even nature itself teach you . . . ?' The word 'learn' of verse 11 shows the other side of this process. The man was to be in the position of teacher—the woman in that of learner, or person taught—thus man was in the superior and dominant position. Compare the thought of Christ as a Son, learning obedience by the things which He suffered. He was subject to the Father. None of this conflicts with the view that a domestic and not particularly a church sphere is envisaged in 1 Timothy 2:11–15.

7 Recent research has shown that the phrase translated 'usurp authority' or 'have dominion' 'does not carry with it the connotation of illicit authority, nor does it carry the connotation of "domineer" ("act imperiously" or "be overbearing") as some translations . . . have suggested. It simply means

"have authority over" or "exercise authority over". What Paul disallowed therefore was simply the exercise of authority over men, which was incompatible with submission, rather than the abuse or usurpation of authority' (Hurley, *Man and Woman in Biblical Perspective*, p. 202).

Hanson writes: 'The literal meaning is "have authority over man", which no doubt means the woman's *husband*' (*The Pastoral Epistles*, p. 72).

There is nothing in all of this to suggest that a woman taking part in a church service and being used of God, for example, in prophecy (which has a teaching component), would be usurping authority. For her to behave in a dominating way at home, however, would breach the rule.

81

10

Beyond Innocency

For many a day I felt the passage we have just considered, to be the most difficult for those taking a strong line in favour of women ministry, but I came to terms with it along the lines indicated in the last chapter. A few years ago, however, I received a fearful jolt. I read again the verse:

> For Adam was first formed, then Eve; and Adam was not beguiled, but the woman being beguiled hath fallen into transgression (1 Tim 2:13).

That, I felt, finished the argument. It seemed that Paul was maintaining that there was in the woman a fundamental weakness that made her inferior to man and that, in addition, she had always been inferior. This did not take the position back to Eden's Fall—but further back to woman in her original creation. It suggested she was a kind of creature who could be beguiled. Adam had sinned with eyes open, which may have been a greater sin than Eve's and for which as head of the partnership he carried full responsibility, but his sin did not suggest a vulnerability to Satanic deception. In short, he may have been more guilty than the woman but she

was viewed as being innately a weaker being. This I
found alarming—I had always considered that redemp-
tion had cancelled the consequences of the Fall and
opened the door for women to be restored to the first
Edenic position. But here was Paul arguing that even in
Eden she was still the weaker vessel and ought to be
under the man's authority.

The shock lasted for almost exactly two minutes and
then came glory. I believe I received very special revelation and insight. It unfolded thus: In Eden, Adam and
Eve were in a condition of innocency. They were untried
and untested. But in the garden God put a tree of which
they might not eat. They were free agents with free
choice, but on one issue there was a clear prohibition.
The hour came when the serpent, seeing his opportunity,
tempted them for his own ends. Now God had put the
tree where it was for His own purposes. He knew the
devices of Satan. He knew that His son Adam would be
tested. I believe, moreover, that He wanted Adam to be
tested. He wanted him to be given an opportunity to
choose 'right' under tempting conditions and surely
when Eve had fallen and eaten the fruit, the pressure on
Adam to join her must have been intense—probably
more so than we realise. I believe that, had Adam overcome, he would have passed from a position of untried
innocency—the condition in which he found himself by
creation —to holiness, a position which would have
resulted from voluntary obedience. The first Adam was
tempted and fell in the first garden. There came another
garden—Gethsemane—and the last Adam faced another
temptation. A cup of exceeding bitterness was put to His
lips and, instead of dashing it undrunk to the ground,
He drained it to the last bitter drop. Where Adam said,
in effect, 'My will not Thine be done,' He said, 'Not

my will but Thine.' The first Adam ate the fruit of the forbidden tree and was not allowed to eat of the tree of Life; the last Adam refused to eat of the tree of disobedience, choosing rather the tree of Calvary, and won for us the right to eat for evermore of the tree of Life. By that one act of perfect obedience to the will of God, He opened the door for all our race to go beyond innocency to holiness. He does not take us back to the Edenic condition. In that condition man was lower than the angels. In the position to which Christ takes us, we are far above angels—'Know ye not that ye shall judge angels?' He makes us heirs of God—joint heirs with Himself. How can we comprehend it? We become part of Himself—His beloved Bride. Part of His body—of which He is Head. We become one with Him as close as a head is to a body, as close as a bride is to a bridegroom—part, surely, of Himself.

Thus the argument of Paul becomes completely understandable if we view the regulations referring to woman's subjection in 1 Timothy 2:12 as applying to the natural life and the domestic sphere. Paul is referring to a creational ordinance which had remained unaltered through the ages and which was to continue to apply in the Church age. Woman, as a natural creature, was still subject to man. But, glory be to God, as a spiritual being the woman in Christ did not merely go back to Eden but went beyond Eden, beyond innocency to a position of holiness with Christ. She gained the right with man to eat of the tree of life—a right which Eve and Adam never had. All the weakness of the woman is swallowed up in the strength of Christ. Her vulnerability is lost in His stability. In this dimension her femininity disappears. This explains why Paul can write to the Galatians that there can be no male and female: for ye all are one man in Christ Jesus (3:28).

A spiritual dimension is envisaged. In another context we read, 'Ye are complete in Him' (AV). The man is complete in Christ—as a man and as an individual and not as part of a company or church. A woman is complete—not as part of man—but as a person with her own separate identity. It is in this relationship with Christ that she functions in public ministry. She is joined to Christ. Christ is alive within her and He is working through her. She and Christ need no other—male or female. Her completion is total. The fact that her first mother was deceived has no significance here. One wonders if those who view her as being fundamentally inferior to man consider that it will forever remain so. Certainly sex division will not appear in heaven and we shall, in that sense, be as angels[1]—but will the passage to Glory affect our basic spirituality or standing with God? In my view, the weakness of the woman in comparison with the man, traceable to Eden, is altered when she comes into union with the God-man at Calvary. Her humanity fades and Christ becomes her strength, her all in all.

This argument, to me, is conclusive. As a functioning spiritual being she is now to be wholly at God's disposal. His Spirit is to be in no way inhibited in her. Finally, we can completely trust the Holy Spirit. He will never unction any woman to do something she ought not to do. That He has mightily unctioned women to engage in the spiritual functions outlined earlier cannot be denied. Their works and God's blessing on them are abundantly evident. The fruit is all around.

Let it be said again. Let it be said loud and clear. 'Set

my people free.' Let the women arise. Let them remove their shackles. Let the mighty host appear.

Note

[1] This does not necessarily mean that there will be no reflection of masculinity or femininity in Heaven.

11

A Helpmeet for Him

Frequent references have been made to woman's subject role in relation to man in the home sphere and it may be that some of my women readers are alarmed and left wondering as to how strong the male domination should be and how the principle outlined ought to be outworked in the lives of Christian couples. In much of this book the concentration has been on woman as a spiritual being, free and independent of man. This chapter is mainly devoted to woman in her secondary role, i.e., in relation to man.

> Wives, be in subjection unto your own husbands, as unto the Lord. For the husband is the head of the wife, as Christ also is the head of the church, being himself the saviour of the body. But as the church is subject to Christ, so let the wives also be to their husbands in everything. . . . Nevertheless do ye also severally love each one his own wife even as himself; and let the wife see that she fear her husband (Eph 5:22–24, 33).

> Wives, be in subjection to your husbands, as is fitting in the Lord. Husbands, love your wives, and be not bitter against them (Col 3:18–19).

> In like manner, ye wives, be in subjection to your own

husbands; that, even if any obey not the word, they may without the word be gained by the behaviour of their wives; beholding your chaste behaviour. . . . For after this manner aforetime the holy women also, who hoped in God, adorned themselves, being in subjection to their own husbands: as Sarah obeyed Abraham, calling him lord: whose children ye now are, if ye do well, and are not put in fear by any terror (1 Pet 3:1–2, 5–6).

To me the woman's role in relation to man seems perfectly simple at one level, but quite profound at another. In the case of ordinary men and women, quite without reference to whether they are in Christ or unconverted, the natural rules governing their relationship are clear-cut. The man has the position of headship in the eyes of God and is regarded as carrying the responsibility that goes with this. Prior to the Fall, Adam and Eve were equal but the headship was vested in the man in the same kind of way as the Father is Head of Christ in the Trinity, although Father and Son are regarded as equal. Now the vast bulk of humanity are unconverted and the natural rules of creation apply regardless of whether or not they are aware of them and obedient to them.

When we come into the Christian world things change. Christ showed what headship really meant. He was Lord and He showed what lordship involved: 'he took a towel, and girded himself. . . . and began to wash the disciples' feet' (Jn 13:4–5). The person who would become great would become servant: 'the Son of man came not to be ministered unto, but to minister' (Mt 20:28). Thus He taught His disciples. The headship of the man over the woman ought to be a headship of loving and caring and serving. Surely this is the way of the 'Servant King'.

Another has written:

Husbands must learn that form of sacrificial leadership which fosters the growth of others. Wives must learn that form of active obedience which is not self-demeaning but joyfully upbuilding. Among fallen humans, even those in whom the image of God is being restored (Col 3:10), this process calls for humility and mutual encouragement.[1]

You may say, 'That is fine in theory but how is it to be outworked in practice? What should a Christian couple do if it doesn't work out?' Now as many as have truly found Christ as Saviour have also taken Him as Lord. We cannot really have salvation without lordship and if He is Lord we are responsible to obey His commandments. What are His commandments to a man in this kind of situation? First, the man is to reckon himself as dead—crucified with Christ—nevertheless alive in another sense. Paul said, 'I have been crucified with Christ; yet I live; and yet no longer I, but Christ liveth in me' (Gal 2:20). Thus the man is to pass to the point of reckoning that Christ is alive within him and living through him. His question to himself as he goes through life is: 'What would Jesus do? Is this, that I am doing, something He would do or something He would approve of my doing?'[2] Honest responses to these questions can greatly alter the way men live. Thus, in his marriage, the man is to know the mind of God and do what Jesus would do or would have him do. In the home, he brings to bear the Divine rule and not the rule of his old fallen nature—which is to be reckoned as crucified and dead. The woman, for her part, is also to be in a similar spiritual relationship to God. Thus if God is the Head of the house and the Head of them both, there should be harmony. If, as often happens, the ideal is not attained—what should they do? Both should be prepared to follow the Christ principle of returning good for evil, turning the other cheek and going the second mile. Love should always prevail—not a selfish desire to get one's own way—right or wrong. There should be consideration one for the other.

The man should very definitely renounce any idea he may have of lording it over his wife as 'the rulers of the Gentiles lord it over them' (Mt 20:25). This is just plain wrong. If the woman follows the leading of God she will in no way want to usurp the position of the man. Rather will she appreciate and accept it. Hurley has written in this connection:

> There are, however, other situations, *not* involving contradiction of biblical teaching, in which husband and wife, even after discussion, prayer and consultation with others, remain irreconcilably committed to different courses of action and are not prepared to give way for the sake of the other. There need not be many such cases, but in a fallen world there will be some. In them, the responsibility of the husband to lead and of the wife to respect his initiative requires her to yield to his decision.
>
> The manner in which such situations are handled is crucial. The husband may not be high-handed and stubborn, knowing that she will finally have to give way. That is not the model of Christ's headship. Neither may the wife be grudging and resentful. That is not the manner of our response to Christ. In the last analysis, when the two can devote no more time to individual and joint seeking of the grace of God to permit them to come to one mind or to be willing to yield to the other, an exchange along the following lines is in order:
>
> Husband: 'Not because I am inherently wiser or more righteous, nor because I am right (although I do believe I am or I would not stand firm), but because it is finally my responsibility before God, we will take the course which I

believe right. If I am being sinfully stubborn, may God forgive me and give me the grace to yield to you.'

Wife: 'Not because I believe you are wiser in this matter (I don't) or more righteous, nor because I accept that you are right (because I don't or I would not oppose you), but because I am a servant of God who has called me to honour your headship, I willingly yield to your decision. If I am wrong, may God show me. If you are wrong, may he give you grace to acknowledge it and to change.'

Such decisions must be made. They can be steps of commitment to God which cement a relationship and assure both partners of the other's loving commitment. They can alternatively be times which show sinful abuse. The sort of commitment outlined above can be used to preserve the dignity and honesty of both partners by setting matters in their proper context.[3]

I found this an interesting quotation and was reminded of an earlier experience of my own as a young teacher. I made a policy decision which affected several of my classes. To me it seemed a straightforward matter of commonsense. My principal teacher, however, on learning of the matter totally disagreed and wanted the position reversed. I thought he was quite wrong and indeed foolishly wrong—but it did not trouble me at all to carry out his wishes. He was in charge of the department and carried the responsibility for it and consequently he had a right to make decisions affecting it. I was serving under him and the 'rightness' or 'wrongness' of my view was quite irrelevant. He could listen to me, which he did. I could express my view strongly, which I did, but, in the end, he was in charge and had the right to make the final decision. I had no ground for complaint. In the same way there will be cases between husband and wife which will be very similar—cases where decision can no longer be delayed and where different views are strongly held. In this sphere the husband carries the final responsibility.

The trouble, however, may not come in just the natural things of life where sensible people often manage to come to an understanding and find a *modus vivendi*. Sometimes harmony is achieved as I heard one man explain: 'I have a very successful marriage. There is never any trouble and there is a fair division of labour. I am the boss. I make all the important decisions and deal with all the major matters like foreign policy, international relations and planning for next century. My wife handles all the minor things, like how much money I should get and what I should do with it, how the rest of our money should be spent, where we should go on holiday and various trivial matters of this kind. It works wonderfully.' Yes, quite! Things, however, are not always as bad as this, although I do suspect that women often get much more of their own way than most men realise. Many a time the man takes a course which he thinks is of his own devising but which, in fact, has been very carefully planned for him by his meek wife. Indeed this maybe even applies to his marriage itself. Women have a wonderful way of quietly getting their own way. As one has said: 'The man may be the head but the woman is the neck and she twists him in whichever direction she chooses.' I must have been very naïve in early days. I remember a lady friend spelling out to me the theory that most men were easily beguiled (what of Eve now?) and really led by their noses by women. 'It is often the woman,' she said, 'who deliberately hooks the man. He never knows it. He thinks he did it himself. Poor soul!' I did not believe it. I had seen no evidence of it—but I respected this lady's powers of perception and acumen and began to observe my acquaintances more closely. I was on a teaching staff at the time and, do you know, I saw the principle in operation within weeks and saw it quickly repeated. Obviously these things had been going on under my nose for years and been quite unobserved.

Where then—apart from natural things, to which both partners in a marriage should consider themselves crucified—may trouble be expected to arise? Simply in the spiritual role where a woman has a right to consider herself totally free of her husband's will or desire. To my mind, there are very clear-cut principles laid down in Scripture. Two duties never clash. Two commands never conflict. Now God has clearly instructed Christians to obey the law of the land, wives to obey their husbands, children to obey their parents—but He has made it equally clear that if obedience to any of these commands conflicts with obedience to Him, the latter is to take precedence. 'Shall we obey man rather than God?' said the disciples as they were forbidden by the rulers of the Jews to preach anymore in the name of Jesus. They went out straight away and preached Christ everywhere. A son must not put father or mother before Christ and Christ made this perfectly clear:

> If any man cometh unto me, and hateth not his own father, and mother, and wife, and children, and brethren, and sisters, yea, and his own life also, he cannot be my disciple (Lk 14:26).

Surely a wife must not put a husband before God if this interferes with her obedience to God. God will never ask her or unction her to do anything out of His will and if a husband interferes in this realm her clear duty is to

93

disobey him and give Christ her first allegiance. If, however, the man does not see things this way there can be trouble. Some may say she should obey the husband in such circumstances but pray that he may change. I do not. I believe she should pray but also that she should give instant obedience to God. She should not wait for her husband unless God gives her freedom to do so. I have always had a great respect for Hudson Taylor, but on one matter have never really agreed with him —his interpretation of the duty of a son or daughter to parents when a position arose where the parents said one thing and God seemed to lead in a different direction. For example, he might be convinced that a person had a genuine call to the mission field but find that parents objected. He was prepared to wait and, if I recollect aright, sometimes wait indefinitely for a change of attitude by the parents before accepting the candidate. I respect his view but do not share it. God makes no mistakes. If He calls He means the call to be obeyed and obedience should not be delayed.[4] Brother Andrew, on the other hand, very strongly teaches an alternative view on a parallel theme. The gospel, he says, must be preached and that to all nations. Some nations, however, say, 'You may not preach the gospel here.' Who is to be obeyed—God or man? 'God,' says Brother Andrew, 'whether it means breaking the law and imprisonment or not.'[5] Where obedience to husbands was concerned, Charles G. Finney very definitely taught that wives should observe this in one sphere but never where the demand of the husband conflicted with the leading of God. In such a case positive disobedience was enjoined.[6] With this view I am in full agreement. The same principles run through all three cases.

To sum up—in the home sphere man is in authority,

but it is an authority characterised by loving and serving. He represents Christ to His wife. She loves and obeys her husband—but her obedience should correspond with her obedience to Christ since the leading of her husband ought to be obtained from Christ in the first place. There should be no clash or conflict of interest. Both should be dead to themselves and alive to Christ. Thus ideally there is provision for perfect harmony. In no case should there be a hard human domination by the man. In no instance is woman's freedom as a spiritual being to be infringed. She has two roles and she is to fulfil them both.

Perhaps to close the chapter a quotation from *Issues Facing Christians Today* by John Stott would be most apposite.

Commenting on the special creation of Eve, Matthew Henry writes with quaint profundity that she was 'not made out of his head to top him, nor out of his feet to be trampled upon by him, but out of his side to be equal with him, under his arm to be protected and near his heart to be beloved'. Perhaps he got this idea from Peter Lombard who in about AD 1157, just before becoming Bishop of Paris, wrote in his *Book of Sentences:* 'Eve was not taken from the feet of Adam to be his slave, nor from his head to be his lord, but from his side to be his partner.'[7]

Notes

[1] Hurley, *Man and Woman in Biblical Perspective*, p.149.
[2] These guidelines are really for a very early stage in Christian experience. After the Baptism in the Spirit, Christians should have clear inner witness of Divine guidance. As they live in the Spirit and are led by the Spirit they should pass from the

childhood stage to a more mature level. We are responsible to know the mind of God and to live in such a way that we do know it.

[3] Hurley, *Man and Woman in Biblical Perspective*, p.151.

[4] Hudson Taylor sought to honour God by obeying and encouraging others to obey the commands 'Honour thy father and thy mother' and, again, 'Children, obey your parents'. He believed that if he honoured God by keeping these precepts God could and would bring circumstances into line—altering, if necessary, the minds of parents. I feel quite self-conscious about disagreeing in this matter with this man who was so greatly used of God, but I must not fall into the fallacy of 'argumentum ad hominem' where an argument is unsoundly based on the character of an individual.

[5] It is interesting to observe the way Brother Andrew, God's smuggler, has regarded law-breaking. His actions are quite deliberate. He has been prepared to enter closed lands quite illegally and to smuggle in forbidden literature. He has reckoned that the command of Christ to go into all the world and preach takes precedence over any human command that forbids this. Interestingly, he has not taken the attitude that God has told us to obey the law and that we should do this until, through prayer, or otherwise, God changes the circumstances. I feel Scripture is on our brother's side on this.

[6] In his autobiography Finney speaks of the case of a husband who violently opposed his wife as she began to seek salvation. He writes: 'She then called to see me, and asked my advice with regard to what course she should take. I told her that her first obligation was to God; that she was undoubtedly under obligation to obey His commands, even if they conflicted with the commands of her husband; and that, while I advised her to avoid giving him offence if she could, and do her duty to God, still in no case to omit, what she regarded as her duty to God, for the sake of complying with his wishes.' Finney goes on to tell of the extreme danger into which this brought her. After she found salvation her husband attempted

to kill her. In the first instance he pursued her with a dagger but she managed to escape from the house. On her return in the morning he again drew the dagger and managed to corner her. She dropped to her knees crying for mercy for herself and for him. Finney continues: 'At this point God arrested him. She said he looked at her for a moment, dropped his dagger, and fell upon the floor and cried for mercy himself. He then and there broke down, confessed his sins to God and to her; and begged God, and begged her, to forgive him.' Quite evidently Finney totally approved of her actions and attitude even to the point of death! (Extracts from *Charles G. Finney: An Autobiography* [Fleming H. Revell Company, 1876], pp. 242–244.)

7 Stott, *Issues Facing Christians Today*, p. 243.

12

The Last Word

I would like to summarise some of the important points
which have emerged from our study and from them
draw conclusions which will seem convincing to unbiased
minds.

In the Old Testament women are seen as subject to
men in domestic and family relations, but independent
in relation to God. Initially, Eve was equal with Adam
although his was the headship. With the Fall, the man
was given dominion and there was no longer the earlier
equality.

From Adam's day through the era of patriarchs and
prophets right to the close of the Old Testament period,
this position remained. At home, man was in control. In
spiritual matters, woman had a life of her own. There
were prophetesses—Miriam, Deborah, Huldah. There
was a woman judge—Deborah. There was even a ruling
Queen (although in a sense she may have been a
usurper). Women were respected and involved in the
worship and religious life of Israel.

During the period between the Old and New Testa-
ments the position changed. Women were downgraded
and treated contemptuously by many men, including
religious leaders. They were not even regarded as being

fit to be instructed by men in the law, far less to give instruction to men. Divorce was light and easy. In brief, they were often regarded as the chattels of men.

The coming of Christ changed all this. With Him came a new dawn. He treated women with love and gentleness. He restored their dignity. Women were numbered amongst His followers and He delighted to teach them spiritual truth. He gained their love and loyalty in return. Not only did a group of them minister to Him of their substance, but when it came to His death they figured prominently and were faithful to the end. Having followed Him from Galilee to Jerusalem they waited round His cross. They prepared spices to embalm His body. It was to a woman He first appeared on resurrection ground. He commissioned that same woman, Mary Magdalene, to be the first witness of His resurrection and to her He gave instructions to reveal His coming ascension. He sent her to announce these things to men.

As we move further into the New Testament we again come on prophetesses (such as the four daughters of Philip), women teachers (e.g. Priscilla), women missionaries (Paul's fellow labourers, e.g., Priscilla, Syntyche, Euodia), women deacons (e.g. Phoebe), women elders (as in letters to Titus and Timothy) and possibly even a woman apostle (Junia).

We observed that the reference to public worship in 1 Corinthians 11 viewed women as participating, and the reference to her being silent in 1 Corinthians 14 in no way contradicted this.

In Romans 8, we noted that in Christ there is no male and female, and when this insight was applied to Paul's instruction to Timothy regarding women teaching we concluded that he was not referring to the kind of teaching in which prophetesses, or women such as

Priscilla, were involved. The 'teaching' referred to implied a usurping of authority, of which a dominant woman could be guilty in a domestic situation.

The loving relationship which should exist in a Christian union has been observed and spheres of authority and obedience defined.

Over all, the general principle has run consistently throughout Scripture. In the natural sphere, woman is subject to man. In the spiritual world, she is totally free. The cross did not merely restore her to the Edenic position of innocency, but took her beyond innocency to holiness. In her completion in Him any innate weakness and vulnerability are removed. In Christ, she reaches (as do men) a higher plane than Adam ever knew.

Now I am well aware that some of my readers may not be prepared to accept all the points that this book presents and may indeed resent some of them; but there may be others who would love to be convinced yet who remain genuinely doubtful if God really does want women in public places preaching to men and, in the course of preaching, inevitably teaching. Is there anything further I have to say to them? Yes indeed, there is still a further line for consideration.

I remember from my school days a form of proof occasionally employed in geometry. It was not a type of proof that mathematicians really favoured, but there were certain propositions which were very difficult to prove by normal methods. In these exceptional cases a negative type of approach was adopted. In seeking to prove, for example, that a particular line must pass through a particular point in given circumstances, and finding this impossible by positive methods, it was supposed that the line passed through any other point, and the consequences were observed. These were always impossible and, generally, positively ridiculous. This then led to the conclusion that the line must therefore always pass through the point indicated.

Let us apply this type of reasoning to our problem. Firstly, if my interpretation of 'silence' and 'teaching' and 'preaching' is correct no problems arise with other parts of Scripture—but let us suppose that I am mistaken and that the opponents of women ministry have interpreted 1 Corinthians 14 and 1 Timothy 2 correctly, taking the view that the latter applies to the church sphere in such a way that women should be totally silent and neither preach nor teach. Where does this take us? If we accept this interpretation of the passages, and particularly the rigid interpretation of the more extreme opponents of women ministry, it takes us to an intolerable and quite untenable position. If I may refer again to the mathematical analogy, I think we will find, as the mathematicians did, that the line has to pass through the given point because of the absurd consequences which result if it does not. What then are the intolerable consequences? I suggest that:

—Joel is found predicting what ought never to have happened—women prophesying.

—Philip's four daughters were doing wrong in this also.

—The women ought not to have spoken in tongues in the upper room.

—Priscilla was gravely mistaken in instructing Apollos.

—The women who were Paul's fellow labourers would have been better to have stayed at home.

—Paul was mistaken when he wrote that in Christ there is no male and female.

—The host of women who publish the tidings simply disappears.

—While a Christian woman is expected to win her unsaved husband she may not teach him the way of salvation.

—Women missionaries, who far outnumber men, ought not to speak to men of the things of God. They had better come home and, may I say it reverently, 'If this is so, God help the lost!'

—A mother may not instruct a teenage son in the way of the Lord, nor a nurse a male patient, nor a woman a Sunday School class with teenage boys present.

Surely the position becomes increasingly ludicrous. Surely the line must pass through the point. Surely women must have freedom to be fully vocal in the service of their Master.

Finally, and this is of most vital significance: God Himself unctions women. Through them the Holy Spirit has drawn tens of thousands if not millions to Christ. They have been, and are being, gloriously used. If God does it, who can gainsay it? This, to me, is the critical and final argument. It is indeed the last word.

Author's Personal Message

May God bless all my readers and, in this case, women in particular. There is such untapped potential amongst you. My heart longs for your full liberation. Through most of a lifetime God has given me a particular ability to recognise potential. My heart leaps when I find it. In so many of you it is so great and so little tapped. O yes, you do serve God. You are *allowed* to give testimony occasionally. May God forgive us—'*allowed*'! In a right situation you would be encouraged, or rather pushed, to exercise your gift and calling to the fullest. It takes so long for prejudice to change. So frequently even in comparatively liberated circles we find situations where you participate when there is a shortage of men. You are 'allowed' to take part as though you were second class citizens. What I really advocate is something far more radical—it is nothing less than that you be encouraged to think of yourselves as being as fully responsible as men to engage in the work of God. Prejudice must be removed from your own minds as well as from the minds of men. Frequently your own self-deprecation is one of your greatest stumbling blocks. If the inner attitude, the inner thinking, the inheritance of ages of suppression, can be changed —the world will shake with the change.

Surely the closing of your mouths has been one of Satan's greatest triumphs. Remember, you form the vast majority of the Church. To have so many of you silenced has been a master stroke of the Enemy.

Ladies, as you will one day stand before God and give an account of the deeds done in the body, consider seriously the question of your calling and your ministry. The question is not, 'What does man allow?' but rather, 'what does God expect and require of me?' I want the inner attitude of vast numbers to change. I want you to be genuinely and fully open to what God has for you. I would stir your faith to grasp the possibilities. In honesty, go before God and be prepared to know His will.

I would close with the words of a woman—she who was highly favoured amongst women, Mary herself, the mother of Christ: 'Whatsoever He saith unto you, do it.'

PART II
ONE LADY'S TESTIMONY

Author's Introduction

I have decided to include the testimony of one lady
through whom God has worked remarkably. She has
been used to bring untold numbers into the Baptism in
the Spirit. Indeed in my early days when I had no
ministry in that direction I made a point of bringing
interested enquirers into gatherings where I knew she
would be present so that they might receive. I had
noticed that while many people laid hands on others few
received through them—but in her case the ministry was
wonderfully effective. A dozen might be seeking and
various people ministering. I noticed that those to whom
she went received. I realised from the beginning that a
very rare gift was in operation.

In addition I noticed that God used her to impart gifts
to others, including myself. Her main ministry has been
to the church and its upbuilding. She has had a profound
effect on many lives. Always a visionary, she has had
constant foreknowledge of coming events and of the
needs of the church. She has carried a burden of prayer
through a lifetime.

At first Miss Taylor found great difficulty in taking
part in public ministry but by the time I first met her
God had dealt with this. It may be that she never found

speaking easy from a natural point of view but she knew
the mantling of God on her ministry. I can never forget
the first time I heard her speak. She was quite unknown
to me and was behind me in a church service. I heard a
voice in prophecy. I had been baptised in the Spirit a
few days previously and I received a profound shock.
The utterance was glorious and the language beautiful
and there opened for me the knowledge that there was
a depth of love possible between the soul and God of
which I had had no previous knowledge. It affected me
greatly.

I was not alone in being affected by Miss Taylor's
prophetic ministry. Many people all over the country
have drunk at that fountain and known its sweetness. In
spite of this, however, she was still reluctant to preach,
but, as God had commanded her to pray and prophesy,
so He dealt with her Himself on this issue and she
ultimately obeyed—again to the blessing of untold
numbers.

In her later days she has been particularly used in
deliverance. She is in many ways a gentle person, and
yet again and again I have known demons come
screaming out of people as she has ministered. They
quite clearly recognise her authority in God and are
compelled to obey God in her. Through her I received
my own ministry of bringing others into the Baptism in
the Spirit. In a similar way I came into the deliverance
ministry. As she has prophesied in a group I have known
the presence of God come upon me as a mantle and
predictions made in such an hour have been remarkably
fulfilled with lifelong consequences. On one occasion I
was clearly identified and it was as though a cloak came
over my head and shoulders. I received a clear call to
preach and I found that fear, of which I had never

previously been conscious, was rooted out of my being. I left that gathering with a fervent urge to preach the gospel. A work began then which continued for years. Indeed it has never ended.

Now an old lady, partly incapacitated as a result of a stroke suffered a few years ago, Miss Taylor can no longer regularly attend church—but she is still active in spiritual work at home. I am helping her to put her testimony on paper. Indeed I am writing much of it on her behalf and checking with her for accuracy. The story is hers but some (though not all) of the words are mine. I have managed to get some parts in her own language. Some of my friends were disappointed when in a first draft more of her own wording had not been included. I am sure many readers will understand this, having themselves been greatly blessed over the years by the richness of Miss Taylor's unique gift of expression which was marked both by its sensitivity and spirituality, but it is not so easy for her now to write or preach. I have circumvented the difficulty to some extent by using a taped message given some years ago. When I come to her own words I use italics.

In the story that follows Miss Taylor shares some of her remarkable experiences of God and of her conflicts with Satan, of visions and exorcisms. She has always been a very private person and has tended to be reluctant to speak about many of her inner experiences. She has been careful not to draw attention to herself, but for the good of a wider world she has been prevailed upon to share some of her treasures. I trust that her story will encourage many others of her own sex to move out publicly for God. She faced the battle they face and God has been with her in power.

13

The Hour of Salvation

The writing of my testimony has been Mr Black's idea, not mine, but I have felt God to be in the matter and trust that what I have to say may be to the benefit of others, particularly to those whom God may be drawing into His service.

As a child I had the privilege of being much in the company of a very godly grandmother who had a remarkable relationship with Christ. To her He was a personal friend always present. Her circumstances were difficult, her husband being unsaved and addicted to drink. However, she bore her burdens bravely and perhaps they helped her to develop a very deep and close walk with Christ. I often stayed at her home and frequently heard her speak to Him and the sense of His reality really pervaded my being in those early years. He seemed to me to be so unutterably lovely and I loved Him deeply. The years passed, my grandmother died and tragedy hit our own family. When I was eleven my dearly loved father suddenly died, leaving my mother with four young children, the oldest of whom was only fifteen. We were heartbroken and knew real poverty. There were days when there was no food in the house. Sometimes my mother and I went without to let my brothers have something. I became aware of my mother's sufferings and there came a time when things were particularly difficult for us. *I stood in the kitchen and I looked out of the window into the sky—it was very blue—and I looked with a rebellious heart. I said, 'God, I don't believe you exist. I don't believe there is a God. If there is a God, He's a monster.' And something entered into my being, a bitterness, a bitterness of gall. It was as though a blackness came into my life. I was still a child, comparatively speaking; still at school. I hated God. I didn't hate Christ: I just . . . put Him away. And the blackness and the darkness came into my life, into my being, for a number of years. I would not listen to anything about God; I wouldn't read a book that mentioned His Name.*

The years passed and I had no thought of ever changing, but one day my youngest brother came in and announced that he was going to the local town hall to hear an evangelist who had started a series of meetings. I was totally uninterested but my brother waxed enthusiastic, going night by night. Ultimately my mother's interest was aroused and she wanted to go too, but being a very shy person she wanted me to accompany her. I had no objection to doing this for her—but I was totally uninterested in the meetings. Night by night I sat through them unaffected. The meetings had evidently started with about a dozen people in a vast hall, but the evangelist, the late Mr George Jeffreys, founder of the Elim movement, quietly indicated that in a short time people would be unable to get in. A man I later knew heard and laughed at this seeming absurdity. Indeed, he felt that there was almost a blasphemous element in what Mr Jeffreys said but he lived to learn his mistake. The place became thronged. People came in their thousands. They came from shipyards, factories and shops, queuing up straight from their work, fearful of not gaining admittance. Many were gloriously converted and healing was a feature of the meetings. For my mother's sake I was in the meetings but *I was rebellious. I was angry; I did what many folks do in meetings. When Mr. Jeffreys began to speak, I switched off. And I switched off night after night after night after night, until his time in Greenock was almost finished. I didn't know a word that had come out of his mouth; I wouldn't listen to the singing. I was the personification of rebellion.*

On the last night of his being in the town, my mother's sister was dying and my mother couldn't go to the service. I didn't know why I did it, but I went alone. I didn't want to go, but under some sort of compulsion, I arrived in the town hall all by myself. That night God broke through my wall of defence. I can't remember what was preached—I haven't the faintest idea. As a matter of fact it was years afterwards before I knew the identity of the person who preached on that night. It was blotted out. I came under conviction, fearful conviction of having denied God. It was the paramount conviction—I had denied the existence of God, I had denied the goodness of God, I had rebelled against Him. Quickly, real agony came upon me. Suddenly I was face to face with the God whose existence I had denied. I don't know how I got home. But I got into the house, put my head into the room where the family were, and said, 'I'm home, I'm just going into my room,' and disappeared immediately.

In two seconds I was flat on the floor crying to God. I sensed I was unclean, unclean to a degree that was insupportable. But above all was this knowledge: God is. *This One, Whom I thought I could obliterate by denying His existence, manifested Himself to me, to my inner consciousness. And the terror of that filled my being—the terror of being in the presence of a Holy God, Whose wrath was toward me in my sin, in my rebellion. I was on that floor for a very considerable time. The carpet was soaked with my crying, with my tears. I was in agony. Before me, in my inner vision, I could see a fearful beam of light, a destroying beam of light. I was terrified that it would shine upon me directly because I knew I would be completely burned up. It was the uncreated beam of light, which comes from God.*

For a moment or two after that, God put me over hell. I realised that hell is ultimate and absolute and eternal separation from God. It is as though two parts of a whole are wrenched apart and never come together again. There is a sense of total incompleteness and agony. Hell is torment, a torment which cannot be described in our human tongue. It is torment indescribable, unutterable, insupportable. Had it gone on for another minute I would have been totally consumed with the agony and the terror of it. I lay there. I didn't know what I could ask for. I knew I had rebelled against God; I had no right to ask God for forgiveness: I had deliberately, consciously, wilfully denied God. Through my grandmother I knew of Him, I had loved Him; I knew Christ, I had loved Him. And I had deliberately denied and hated God. I had given up any hope of reconciliation. I had accepted this state as being mine for time and for eternity.

I got past the point of being able to utter a cry, so deep was the anguish, so deep was the reality of this hell, which I thought was my destiny. Then, between that awful light, that destroying blaze (I couldn't lift up my head, and yet it penetrated into the darkness), between that and myself, there came a shimmer, an orb of translucent light, gentle, pure. And I realised it was the Risen Christ. Not as Jesus of Nazareth, not as a man, but the Lord Jesus Christ, robed in light as we might remember from the Transfiguration scene. He was light. He was transparent in purity, in love, in

113

gentleness and kindness. I sensed a warmth, a tenderness. And He touched me. There passed through my whole being a fire, a cleansing fire, a fire that burned from my mind into my emotion, to my heart, into my whole being. And I lay there spent, but I could cry, 'I'm clean, I'm clean! O God, I'm clean.' And there was union with God: not a God of wrath, not a God of frightful condemnation, but a God of forgiveness, Who was also the God of holiness.

I was born again under one who was anointed of the Holy Spirit, under the preaching of one who had come up from the Welsh Revival. I didn't realise at the time that I was born again in revival fire. The power of God that came upon me to convert me was the fire that had burned in revival so long before I was born. But one had been faithful, and another one had been faithful, and the torch of that revival was carried through into my own day, into my own life. The revival fire burned within myself from that moment. My life was transformed. There was born within me a passionate love for the Lord Jesus Christ, a love which is beyond telling, a love which is stronger than death, a love that drives on for Christ's sake, for Christ's sake. God has wrought miracle after miracle in my life. And it is all for love of Christ. There was such a passionate love born in me in these moments of conversion. There came into my being in that experience a knowledge of Who God is: He is the Lord God of Hosts, Almighty, before Whom no man can stand. He is the Living God: beside Him there is no other. I tell you, there never was any thought of anything irreverent in me, and there certainly never was after that moment. I saw God in Christ. I saw Christ, the Son of God, and there was created within my being a fire, a fire of love, for the Godhead. Through a long lifetime, that fire has burned stronger and stronger, and deeper and deeper. It never faded. It was never diminished. In my worst times, that love has been constant. It's the love *of God. It's not my love, it's the love of God. That is conversion! You come out of where you were, into a totally new sphere of living. You come into a conscious knowledge of the Godhead. He is not someone we can disregard. What He says is law. What He says, we must obey or abide the consequence.*

14

The Enduement with Power

I'll just touch on my Baptism. You see, at the time of my conversion there was such an incoming of the Triune God in the locality that the Baptism was being poured out on hundreds of people. But it was such an astonishment to me that God had saved me, that God had lifted this rebel, this almost-blasphemer, and had cleansed and reinstated me, had put me into a place where I could speak with God—I thought there was no more God could, or should, give me: I expected nothing else. To have received that was tremendous. I never asked to be baptised: I didn't dare. I thought I could never ask for more than I had received. But there came a moment in my own home when God baptised me at my mother's bedside . . . but she didn't hear me, it was so gentle a whisper, it was so quiet. But it was fire. It was dynamite. A small piece of dynamite can cause a tremendous explosion. And that quiet experience became a raging inferno of fire within my being. It touched all the experience of the new birth, brought it all into fullness. And so through the years, God has again and again and again and again put fuel on that fire. O Glory to His Name!

O child of God, enter into the new birth. Enter into it. If you have been saved at a light level, seek God until you are converted. Seek that deep awareness, knowledge, revelation of the Godhead Three—seek it until you find Him and know Him, not that you know you are saved, but you know the One Who has saved you. It transforms life, every moment of life, secular and sacred, until there is only one life, and that is a sacred living in God. It's strong, it's mighty strong, it's powerful, it's stronger than Satan, stronger than sin. It's stronger than every circumstance that can come against the life. If you are born again of God, truly born again, truly changed, you will be converted into a new creature—I tell you, there was never a moment's flicker of doubt: I became a new creature. I didn't make myself a new creature, I became a new creature, by the new birth. Oh, I grieve, I grieve, for I see so many who just don't know what it's about. So many don't really know what it means to be saved. They don't know what it is to be saved. They think, 'It's something . . . but I don't know what.' I tell you: I knew. I was saved from hell. I was saved from the wrath of Almighty God. I was saved to peace with that God. It's real. It's very real. And so also is the Baptism: the fire of God. 'Ye shall receive power, after that the Holy Ghost is come upon you.' 'He shall baptise you with the Holy Ghost and with fire.' Fire. It doesn't have to be a great, terrific occasion. It might be. It doesn't have to be. It just has to be real. The shallowness that is in the church of Christ is an insult to the Blood of Christ. The shallowness of conversion that is accepted is an insult to the power of the Holy Spirit. Oh that all who have opportunity to speak to others of salvation would be careful not to make it cheap. Don't make it light. It is life-changing, for all of life, not just for a few days. I thank God, He changed me. I thank God the fire of the Holy Ghost has burned from the moment of my conversion. It transcends every human desire, every human thought, every human effort. All these are superimposed upon, by the power of God, by love for God. Love for God will make you do anything God asks you to do.

15

Facing the World

I loved Him on the night He saved me. With the Baptism
came an ever deepening love. Into a home which had
known deep pain and sorrow, love had come, and now
came a wonderful joy. The Baptism had a profound
effect. It greatly deepened my spiritual life. There was
a constant flow of love towards God and a knowing of
His presence and power. There was unbroken communication—but He did not change my basic temperament.
There had been a time when I suffered from a violent
temper and this and other aspects of my life He dealt
with—but not my temperament. I was a very reserved
person—inordinately shy. Indeed I suffered so much
from this that I found it difficult to go into a shop to do
ordinary shopping. It was an ordeal for me to meet new
people. I had always been like that. The characteristic
was inherited from my mother. It was in the warp and
woof of my being and it did not change with my new
experience. The essential me was still painfully reserved.
Then came an awful moment. God asked me, quite
clearly asked me, to pray publicly at the communion
services. I could not do it. I just could not do it. I
refused. To me it was a sheer impossibility but God
persisted and ultimately it came to a question of costly

obedience or deliberate disobedience and in desperation I yielded. Then came the moment. We were gathered for worship and we were a large company. The minister's wife who had a beautiful gift of prayer and prophecy stood to take part. It was beautiful and I immediately reacted, 'I just can't stand up after that.' Then a very rough diamond of a man with an Irish brogue rose and thanked God in a very brief, simple and sincere way for his salvation and sat down. The simplicity of this greatly affected me. Both prayers had been wonderful but in markedly different ways. The second encouraged me to obey God. I was able to get to my feet and said, 'O God'—and then I fainted. It was a beginning. It was very difficult—but I did it. It never became easy from a natural point of view but my temperament compelled me to become dependent on God and when His mantle came my weakness was swallowed up in His strength and by His power I have gone on.

There came a day when our minister had a call to another charge and we were to lose both him and his wife. He was a true man of God with real spiritual discernment. His wife was the only one in the church with the gift of prophecy and their going was a serious loss. One day there came a knock on my door and the minister indicated that he had come to see me. God had instructed him to lay hands on me for the receiving of the gift of prophecy. He simply obeyed and I received the gift in that hour. From that day it has been in operation. I knew from the beginning that I had to keep myself reserved to God—not to be involved in the normal social round, knowing the gossip of the people. I must be apart for His service and in tune at all times for His purposes. To fulfil the prophetic ministry it was essential for me to live this way. It was particularly important not to know at natural levels much of what was going on, so that I would be unbiased and the word that I spoke would be the pure word of God. I did not condemn others who were not called to walk this way, but I knew that there were many ordinary things in life that seemed to be permissible to others, which were forbidden to me. My life became deeply separated to God: it became a life of prayer and care and intercession.

Time passed and I was regularly used in public prophecy and I had revelation of hidden things. At an earlier stage, I had had a vision of the town in flames and the people fleeing to the hills. This was publicly predicted some years before war broke out. The vision was wholly fulfilled. There came a night when Greenock was blitzed. The distillery blazed with fire and much of the town burned. The place became a raging inferno. The people fled to the hills. We spent the night in a strutted close* with bombs raining down all around. A land mine came down about fifty yards from where we were, destroying a large property and killing many people. Throughout that long night God came through me in ministry to others. It came through a ceaseless flow of remembered Scriptures, which was in itself a miracle since I have a poor memory. [The author is not so sure about this but knows what Miss Taylor means. Maybe naturally her memory is bad, but under the Spirit it is remarkably good.] Even unbelievers were affected. There came a quietness, almost a fearlessness. He was

* For non-Scottish readers, I should explain that a close is the ground floor entrance to a tenement building. Much of the housing in Scotland was previously of this type. To provide air raid shelter during the last war, these were often strutted, i.e. reinforced with corrugated iron.—*Author*.

there all the time. In the morning we left the shelter and looked up at the house. The gable wall was a hole. Part of the roof had collapsed. The house was largely wrecked and we were left with nothing—no home, no goods, no money—but there was no consciousness of loss, just of the presence of God. The sense of His presence was so great that it eclipsed any sense of loss there might have been. He gave quietness and confidence. The words of Christ were fulfilled, 'My peace I give unto you—My peace.' God indeed was faithful and in wonderful ways made provision for us. He prevented the demolition of the house. Most other houses in the condition ours was in were levelled to the ground—but ours was rebuilt and restored. He took care of us in every way in those difficult days.

The years passed and there came a time when God clearly indicated to me that He wanted to start a particular work. He showed me the standard of holiness and separation He desired and the type of work He planned. He asked me to go forward for Him. I pleaded an inability to take public leadership and asked for an Aaron to help as He had allowed Moses. He granted my request and the work began. Through that work today there are churches in various parts of the country, untold numbers of people saved, baptised in the Spirit, healed and delivered from demon power. God has been entirely faithful, although we at times have failed Him. He has been true to His every promise.

I have been asked to speak about myself and this is not always easy. My own life was lived much in the hidden place. Through domestic circumstances I was much confined for years—but God was powerfully with me and I suppose ministries deepened and developed. As I go on to speak of experiences and realms of ministry it is impossible to conceal myself completely, but I want readers to understand that any effective action through me came from God. If there is glory it is all His. For my failures I am entirely responsible.

I have been particularly asked to write of inner things and I have always been reluctant to say too much about this realm of life, which has been very much between myself and God. On the other hand, I have benefited from the lives of people such as Madame Guyon, and it may be that my experiences will be of value to others. I am also conscious of my own disappointment with many biographies. They present highlights of life, times of joy and victory, and are peculiarly silent about dark days. So often they seem divorced from reality and so unlike life as I know it. Now I am in the position of writing and I can understand that there are good things to share that can encourage others—but I have also memories of times of deep pain and difficulty that lie between God and me. Many of these are private. I will make allusion to them so that others may know that life, even Christian life, has shade as well as light. There is a 'dark night of the soul,' and people who come through it often go on into the deeps of God. So such times will be alluded to, but readers should know that all is not revealed in either the realms of glory and success or of pain and failure.

There are eight areas in particular about which I have been asked to comment: the relationship of the soul with God, spiritual warfare and exorcism, 'the dark night of the soul,' the power of binding and loosing, the love of Christ, the realm of vision and revelation, sickness in the life of Christians, and the ministry of women.

16

The Relationship of the Soul with God

This is of vital importance and should never be regarded casually. It is fundamental. There is a place of intimacy with Christ where He is adored—a tie between the soul and God. When this is strong, miracle happens all around. The life becomes immersed in God and words spoken, whether publicly or privately, have a powerful effect on other lives. The work of God takes root and frequently gifts of the Spirit operate powerfully. God's servant must resist the temptation at this point to focus attention on the work and take it off Christ. Even God's work can be a distraction and can be wrongly viewed. Christ is forever the centre and work should be an over-flow from a relationship between the soul and God and be wrought by the power of the Spirit. Guard the inner place with Christ. Make Him always the sanctuary of the soul. This is of primary and not secondary importance.

[*Author's Note*: When I was going over my writing with Miss Taylor she paused, evidently not totally satisfied by how I had expressed certain points and, with that look into another world which will be so well remembered by many readers, commented,] *It is very difficult to convey deep spiritual truths in words. How can you really do it?* [I asked her about her views on the relationship of the soul with God and on spiritual warfare, and she said:] *The strength of the ministry is the unassailable knowledge of the supremacy of Christ over Satan. The supremacy of Christ is a fact. At this moment Satan is grinding his teeth that others are going to read this. Christ bound the strong man and we are sent to spoil his goods. It all springs from our spiritual relationship with God: the quality of it and the intensity of it. He brings a tranquillity into the mind and spirit that are unassailable. It is His gift to those that are resting in Him.*

17

Spiritual Warfare and Exorcism

I came through a period in my life which is almost indescribable. Without warning and without knowledge that such things could happen, evil powers came against me. I had known this in the normal sense of these words, but this was different. They actually literally invaded my room. They were as real as people might have been had they come in physically. They made themselves manifest in physical ways. They tried to terrify me. Night by night for long periods this persisted until I learned something of the power of Christ. They never succeeded in their assaults. Christ always intervened until I gained a total confidence in His power and a total fearlessness of Satan and all his works. I saw the wicked one defeated in the spiritual world and was prepared for his defeat in the world of men. I was later to learn that others have had similar experiences, for example Madame Guyon. After trying to destroy her unsuccessfully in one way, Satan switched tactics and came in other ways—shaking her windows and causing physical manifestations of his presence. She too remained unmoved and her life deepened in God. This training was of vital importance to me—my backbone became like steel. I hated the enemy and was strengthened of God to destroy his kingdom.

Let me say again, the teaching of Christ should be remembered. The strong man has to be bound before his goods are taken. I was to find God leading me into ministry against that evil kingdom—against both Satan and his minions.

There are two areas of war with Satan of which I want to speak; the general warfare which is 'not against flesh and blood, but against the principalities, against the powers, against the world-rulers of this darkness, against the spiritual hosts of wickedness in the heavenly places,' and secondly the more particular war against demon entities, resulting in exorcisms. Every Christian is called on to do battle with evil. For this purpose we require 'the whole armour of God.' Many people find themselves tormented by evil largely because of the practices in which they indulge. It is a case of spending a lifetime repelling boarders. Others advance from that position and find they are opposed by Satan as they labour on behalf of others. Paul knew this realm. He knew that there were powers of darkness that held sway over particular lives, over communities and over whole lands—principalities and powers; spiritual rulers of darkness. This is extremely real. Again and again I have had to go against Satan, not only over individual lives, but on behalf of communities and situations. He is very real. I have known revelation of his grip on a town and on a country and have had to do battle with him on these issues. I have known a case where I came against evil spirits which had been in a person's ancestors in a distant land. They were seeking to destroy a life which had been given to God. There is a distinct difference between the general wide field of battle with Satan and with the more particular battle with his minions (or himself, for that matter) which results in exorcism and demons being driven from bodies to which they have gained entrance.

Before going in any detail into this, I would like to mention one incident that could be of interest to readers. Around the time of my conversion I worked in a shop and a traveller who was then one of the leading spiritualist mediums in Scotland used to come in. One day he asked me to give him something belonging to me as he wanted 'to read me.' I refused. He persisted and was determined to have his way. He set himself to penetrate my defences—concentrating till perspiration broke on his brow. Finally he gave up, totally baffled, saying he had never met anything like this before. With everybody else he had been able to get inside. I had told him that there was a stronger power in me than there was in him and that he would fail. That man begged me to turn from God and go his way, promising great things. I suppose there is a part us that can be used by God or Satan. For me there was no temptation. Even at that early stage I knew my God. On another occasion a passing gipsy made a very similar request and was very persistent about it. She too was repulsed.

The day came when God took me into the realm of exorcism. What shall I say? I cannot go into all the detail of the years. As the anointing of God comes on me in this ministry I discern evil powers very clearly. Indeed I see them. With the anointing there is both a strength and an anger against evil. The people being dealt with are usually immediately affected and it is often as though a spiritual sickness is manifest. Sometimes as the demons come out people actually are sick. On some occasions demons violently resist the ministry and cry 'with loud voices' as they did in Christ's day. Sometimes they rend and wound as they did then too. On occasion God will not allow them to say a word; sometimes exorcism is very quick and comparatively quiet, and there may be little more than a sigh or a cough. There may not even be that—the action may be completely internal. Frequently, under anointed preaching, or in times when the presence of God is particularly strong, demons simply flee from people. On the other hand, where there is deep possession they can be very difficult to drive out. I have found the ability 'to see' to be of tremendous value. Frequently, when a number of demons are in one individual, one or more will attempt concealment. On one occasion about fourteen had come from a man—each in snake form—but the oldest and strongest was very deep in the personality. It had been there for a very long time. It thought it was hidden but God revealed it to me and ultimately it too was compelled to come up and out. The joy and relief of those delivered is wonderful. I remember one lad who had been tormented for a lifetime with a spirit of fear. When I prayed for him the spirit was revealed as a gigantic monstrosity looming over him. There came a moment when I knew and said that the sword of Christ was in its heart. It collapsed like a deflated balloon. That young man rose radiant with great joy. He said, 'I'm free. There has never been a time in my life since my earliest memory when I have been free from fear—just naked fear. Now it has gone.' He and we glorified God!

On another occasion a doctor sought help. As soon as I set eyes on her a demon within her challenged me and threatened me with death if I moved against it. (This was done in silence.) The lady had previously had horrific psychic experience with physical manifestation but on that day she was gloriously delivered and has remained free. Frequently I have been threatened with death. Indeed it happened about a week before the stroke I suffered some years ago. A particularly powerful and violent demon was driven out of a young man and it struck at me as it went. In no way did I draw back from ministering in the face of the threat. Indeed, threats have again and again almost catapulted me out of my chair to go into attack. I am still alive. My times are in God's hands, not Satan's.

Demons are revealed to me in various forms as I minister—frequently in snake guise, but also as angry bees, as dark polluted liquid affecting the whole of a person's bloodstream, as a grey enveloping mist holding out the light of the sun.

My early experiences in the aloneness of my room have stood me in good stead. I know my enemy and I know my God. My confidence in the power of God over Satan is absolute. I have seen His triumph outworked in bodies of more people than I can remember. I have known a great strong man who, on the very verge of being ministered to, suddenly rose and ran for his life. He told us that voices within him were telling him he would die if he remained for ministry. Voices often tell people this. It is a lie of the devil. On one occasion when a person told Mr Black that he was being threatened with death, Mr Black replied that he would be better dead than continuing with these evil powers inside him, and that it was a lie anyway. He would not die but live, and he did go on to live indeed—free of these powers.

On one occasion a young man who had involved himself in Satanism accompanied a girlfriend who was seeking Christ. The young man was cynical and proud but, in spite of himself, disturbed. He returned later for ministry but the demons fought him. They tried to postpone the critical hour. That young man, I imagine, had previously thought there was no power in Christianity. He was to learn. He fell like a log to the ground shouting on Satan for help. I almost said I could write a book (figuratively speaking), but I suppose I am doing just that—at least part of one! To sum up—Jesus Christ is Lord. I have known it, seen it and proved it. Do seek to minister in the power and demonstration of the Spirit. Enough of demons. Indeed I should perhaps say it is never wise to concentrate too much on the realm of darkness. I never do. Dwell in light—think of pure things. Let God deal with Satan. Never become entangled in his doings. Nor is it wise to speak too much of his activities. It can darken an atmosphere and concentrate attention on him, which he loves. Let your mind dwell on God and the things of God. Then you will remain strong and pure in the work of God. You may feel that I have not followed my own advice in opening up this subject as deeply as I have done, but there are times when it is necessary to expose Satan publicly, as this book is doing now.

18

The Dark Night of the Soul

There is a 'dark night of the soul.' There can come in the purposes of God a time when all the familiar evidences of His love and care are withdrawn from life. Where formerly there was sweet and constant communion, there is a darkness and a deadness and no understanding of the reason why, and many a strong soul has almost broken in such an hour—but it is always wise to trust God even when you cannot understand. I suppose the truth is that when we walk with God and literally feel and enjoy His presence our development may remain only partial:

> But flowers need night's cool darkness,
>   The moonlight and the dew;
> So Christ, from one who loved it,
>   His shining oft withdrew.

God wants us to grow up and to grow strong. He draws the soul out after Him while He, Himself, recedes. He compels us to run after Him. Like the bride in the Song of Solomon we diligently seek the One Whom our soul loves but Who has withdrawn Himself. We learn to trust when we cannot see—to go faithfully on when we cannot feel. We must learn that, as Christ said, 'the flesh profiteth nothing: the words that I speak . . . they are spirit and they are life' (AV). He wants to take us into a totally spiritual dimension and we have to die at a deep level to enter there. There are aspects of the 'dark night' which remain forever mysterious—but let those to whom it comes welcome it. If borne properly it will be to their ultimate good. Remember Norman Grubb. He too went through an incredibly deep darkness but emerged into glorious usefulness. 'All chastening seemeth for the present to be not joyous, but grievous: yet afterward it yieldeth peaceable fruit unto them that have been exercised thereby, even the fruit of righteousness.'

Never confuse the 'dark night' with dark times that come directly as a result of our own folly. It is of quite a different nature. By repentance, one darkness can be turned to light. With the other, which is unconnected with sin, it remains until God's particular work in the soul is complete. An interior life develops. God comes deeply within the soul; it leans on no external props. As these are removed, it goes into darkness—but God finds it as it were in the midst of the darkness and the great truth that 'God is' is revealed to the soul, *and it comes out of the darkness with an unshakable certainty*. In the face of this reality everything else is judged and much for ever disappears. A stage is reached when, like Madame Guyon, the soul may say:

All scenes alike engaging prove
  To souls imprest with sacred love;
Where'er they dwell, they dwell in Thee,
  In heav'n, in earth, or on the sea.

To me remains nor place nor time;
  My country is in every clime;
I can be calm and free from care,
  On any shore, since God is there.

While place we seek, or place we shun,
   The soul finds happiness in none;
But with my God to guide my way,
   'Tis equal joy to go or stay.

Could I be cast where Thou art not,
   That were indeed a dreadful lot:
But regions none remote I call, —
   Secure of finding God in all.

and in the words of another:

My goal is God Himself, not joy, nor peace,
   Nor even blessing, but Himself, my God:
'Tis His to lead me there, not mine but His –
   'At any cost, dear Lord, by any road!'

Seek these places in God. Go through with Him to the deepest depths. There are in Him inexhaustible riches and glory. Become really one with Christ—an heir of God and joint heir with the Beloved.

[On this subject too Miss Taylor made particular comment in her own language.] *The core of the experience was that in any circumstance and every circumstance—no matter how dark things seemed, no matter if there was no evidence of His presence and if things were shaped to deny the existence and truthfulness of God—there was a knowledge within the being of His verity, a knowledge that God is, and is truthful and faithful. Satan would come and, when assaulting the soul, would produce seeming evidence that God did not exist and was not supporting me or giving evidences of His being the manna required. In that moment there came an unquestionable knowledge that without conscious evidences there is the certainty that God is Who He is and is what He says He is. There is no denying the fact of God.*

19

The Power of Binding and Loosing

In the Bible we read that 'Whatsoever things ye shall bind on earth shall be bound in heaven: and whatsoever things ye shall loose on earth shall be loosed in heaven.' The verse is often read but seldom understood. People tend to have vague ideas that these verses were in some undefined way related to the apostles. That they have relevance to our day is not generally known, but is indeed the case.

Some years ago, a Church of Scotland minister spoke publicly of his own experience in this realm; his testimony was remarkable. As a young man, he had been an active communist, and found himself at a meeting in Hyde Park addressed by Dr. Soper. He was present with the deliberate intention of interrupting the meeting. This he proceeded to do by heckling. A point came when Dr. Soper stopped speaking and addressed the young man in words like these: 'In the Name of the Father and the Son and the Holy Spirit, I bid you hold your peace.' Immediately the man was affected. He said, 'I couldn't speak. I couldn't speak one word; and indeed I never spoke again until I was converted in Dr. Soper's vestry.'

That young man had been bound in Hyde Park that day, and what Dr. Soper bound on earth was bound in heaven.

I have known the operation of this gift, if I may call it gift, for many years. The binding side tends to operate if a person is being used of Satan to disrupt the work of God. I receive a quiet command in my spirit: 'Bind that man.' The person doesn't really know what happens to him. It is as though a spiritual rope goes round him—he is tied and cannot go free. He is bound in respect to his mistaken course. He loses power and impetus to go on with it. This can be a very effective and powerful gift.

The power of loosing is a lovely ministry. Satan may have bound a man for many years, and he can be set free through the gospel, a man may be demon-possessed and receive deliverance—but there is almost, I might say, another realm. I have known a person who has committed his life to Christ fall again into a snare of Satan. He had been truly saved, there was no evidence of demon invasion—but he was bound and seemingly could not go free. On one occasion, two young men found themselves in this position at the same time. One had been saved from a dreadful background quite miraculously. Drink had held him in its grip. He backslid, and backslid badly. The other had a very different background. He had been deeply called of God and deeply used of God. In his university days he fell and in his case he too fell badly. There seemed little hope for either of these lives. They were both going downward fast, and there seemed to be no desire in them to alter course. While as yet there was no faintest ripple on the surface indicating a change of attitude I was moving about my own home one day when suddenly, as

I was going into a cupboard, God spoke to me clearly and told me He would give me both of these lives. Something immediately happened in me: I had power in God to loose them from Satan's grip, and I did it. Both returned to their first love, and that very quickly.

The warfare is not against flesh and blood but against Satan—not primarily against human weakness or adverse circumstances or things of that nature, but against spiritual powers of darkness. To deal with these one must operate in a spiritual realm. 'The weapons of our warfare are not carnal,' but spiritual, and they are strong 'to the pulling down of strongholds.' The gift, or ministry, of binding and loosing is a spiritual weapon and is very potent. The intensity of the power that is used in this operation can be almost frightening. It is a vital area to enter—but only seek to go into it, as with exorcism, under Divine covering and guidance.

20

The Love of Christ

Love to me is fundamental. To know Him is to love Him. All our work should be related to that bond. He is to be for ever central. What can I say of love? Surely it is something felt rather than something spoken. It is related to a Person—the altogether lovely One. Take time to know Him. Read His love letters which have been left to all the world. Meditate on His law, on His person. One meets people who don't know what it really is to love Christ. The author of this book often tells people that if they find difficulty in concentrating on spiritual things, if they systematically turn their thoughts to God for two or three days they will find that their minds will begin to swing back to Him automatically when freed from normal matters requiring attention. It then becomes a way of life to dwell constantly in God. When Paul instructed people to pray without ceasing he well knew that the deep mind could dwell on Christ when the surface mind was otherwise occupied. Mr Black also often tells people to begin with fifteen minutes a day and meditate on Christ—to read of Him and simply be in His presence and love Him. Love will quickly come. You cannot know Him without loving Him. I find it difficult to write this section. It is so close to me. Love for Christ is part of me. I cannot, could not live without Him. I want you to know that I am not using these words in a vague theoretic way. It is not a case of 'Christ is God. He died for me. I really ought to love Him, etc. etc.' The truth is, He is 'the chiefest among ten thousand and the altogether lovely one.' To the soul that really knows Him and has fallen in love with Him he is

Fairer than all the earth beside,
  Chiefest of all unto His bride.

To me He is and has been a passion for almost sixty years and this is really true—more beloved by me than any other ever was or is, indeed more than all others put together. This kind of love is at the very heart of true Christianity. God is love. Without love a child can perish. We should be born in love in the natural world. Without it there is no birth in the spiritual world. We develop in love and we journey on to unutterable love. Dwell in love and you will dwell in God.

21

The Realm of Vision and Revelation

From my earliest days in Christ I have been a visionary. I would not normally use this language about myself but Mr Black uses it of me and I suppose it is true. The revelation of God and of Christ was intense at my salvation and through all the years God has revealed Himself in vision as well as in other ways. Frequently I receive vision of the unfolding of other lives—far into the future—of opportunities that will be theirs and of the dangers they face. This is normal and regular—but there are times when more general aspects of the work of God are revealed; for example, on one occasion I had the vision of a fountain pouring up through a particular church. Waters were falling on various parts of the country. I passed the message on to the appropriate person and for years thereafter wherever he went blessing followed with the planting of churches. On another, I had a vision of one church and, springing from it, daughter churches, which would endure till Christ's return. Daughter churches came into being.

I have known God come to a people who refused to hear Him when previously He had given me a vision of a bride bound on an altar, being approached by Christ with a knife in His hand. Her eyes had filled with fear and she refused the sacrifice. She had failed to see that *His* eyes were filled with love. On another occasion when God started a work amongst young people, Christ came into a hall and revealed to me the coming stream of youth. At the same moment, unknown to me, another was receiving practical details about the outworking of the vision. Visions are not sought, nor does one get unduly taken up with them. If God chooses to give them that is well and to His glory, but He Himself must always remain central. Long ago He gave me a vision of revival. When there was no cloud of rain in the sky, He spoke to me of Elijah and the cloud the size of a man's hand and instructed me to pray. The floods are surely coming. I do not expect to live to see it fulfilled, but it will surely come and it will not be long in coming.

May I speak of two more—experiences, perhaps, rather than visions as generally understood. A number of years ago I was critically ill and went down into the valley of death. I discovered that it was not as I had always imagined it—a long narrow valley down which one walks. It was rather a matter of going down the side of a valley which actually runs along beside us all the time although it is normally unseen. I went down and a knowledge of the defilement of sin came over me. I knew Christ but suddenly I knew the need for fresh cleansing. He came, and the robe of His righteousness came upon me. I went on over the valley and up the other side. A light coming from Christ Himself tinged everything with a lovely purple hue. The light grew brighter as I reached the other side. I was almost over and about to enter Heaven when Christ touched me and indicated that my work on earth was not complete and He wanted me to go back. I came to consciousness on earth again. It was God's plan for me, but in one way a fearful disappointment.

More recently, after the time of my stroke I thought I was going home. Again I was in the valley. This time it was a narrow valley down which I went. This time God's glory filled all the exit. He was the terrible God— the God of holiness and power. I became aware that there was no way into Heaven which bypassed God. Without forgiveness of sin through Christ there was no way in. Again, while I rejoiced at what Christ had done for me, I came back to the body with a deeper sense than I had ever known of the God of whom the writer of Hebrews said, 'Our God is a consuming fire.' It was a deeply solemnising experience and I would recommend this aspect of the character of God for your serious thought.

What of the future? Not a seen vision but a glorious hope—no, a glorious knowledge. I shall be satisfied when I awake in His likeness. I shall see Him even as He is:

> The bride eyes not her garment,
>   But her dear bridegroom's face;
> I will not gaze at glory,
>   But on my King of grace;
> Not at the crown He gifteth,
>   But on His pierced hand;
> The Lamb is all the glory
>   In Immanuel's land.

22

Sickness in the Lives of Christians

Readers of the first draft of this book have suggested that I comment more specifically on sickness and the suffering associated with it in the lives of Christians. Through most of a lifetime, I have known a great deal of sickness. God allowed it, and it brought a peculiar discipline into life. Often I had my questions about this. There were times when pain and illness seemed to curtail my usefulness, but I now know that in fact they drove me deeper into God, and enabled Him to deal with parts of my personality which might otherwise have remained unbroken. There are those who teach that there should never be sickness in the church. Ideally this may be so, but just as certainly God has allowed some of His choicest saints to go through the valley of physical suffering. I am not claiming to be numbered in that select category—but remember Madame Guyon, whose sufferings were at times intense, and remember the deeps of God that she found, to the benefit of Christians through the centuries. Frances Ridley Havergal, the saintly author of 'Take my life and let it be/Consecrated, Lord, to Thee,' had a lifetime of illness. She wrote of natural life having times of sorrow and times of joy, and 'more of the first than the last.' Amy Carmichael, founder and leader of the Dohnavur Fellowship, was bedridden for the last twenty years of her life—seemingly put out of active service, but really given opportunity to know God in depth and write books that have brought blessing and a knowledge of God into so many lives.

C. T. Studd, the great cricketer, missionary pioneer and founder of the Worldwide Evangelization Crusade, suffered greatly from various ailments for years. Referred to as 'the graveyard deserter' and finding no doctor or committee to back him because of his ill health, he took God the Father, Son and Holy Spirit as his committee and, leaving an invalid wife to take care of the work in Britain, sailed for Africa. On the voyage there God told him that his mission was not to Africa only, but to the whole unevangelised world. He lived for another twenty years and founded a mighty work for God, with thousands finding Christ. He wrote to his wife from Africa, asking (or perhaps I should say commanding) her to leave her sick bed in faith. With God's help she did just that and loyally and actively supported her husband through the rest of her life. Studd was a great man and the motto he gave his mission is forever memorable: 'If Jesus Christ be God and died for me, then no sacrifice that I can make for Him can be too great.'

Hudson Taylor, too, suffered ill health in his closing years, and that after a life of unusual fruitfulness. Remember the apostle Paul himself: he may not have suffered in this way, but he was imprisoned for many a weary day when he may well have thought that he could have been much better employed in carrying the Gospel all abroad. And yet we who live in a later age have some appreciation of the work God did through him and of the debt we owe him for the epistles which came from prison. John, too, on the Isle of Patmos knew privation and imprisonment, yet from the very heart of the salt mines wrote the glorious Book of Revelation. Surely,

> God moves in a mysterious way
>> His wonders to perform.
>
> He plants His footsteps in the sea
>> And rides upon the storm.

Frequently He comes to His saints on the wings of storm.

Throughout my own life God has allowed severe pressure again and again, and this has driven me into deep dependence on Him. I remember a period when this was lifted, but I noticed that there was at the same time a waning of spiritual life, until I begged God to bring back the pressure. In this matter I took up my cross and followed Him. He heard my cry, and restored me to a place of fruitfulness.

When the pressure was lifted from me. I couldn't live in the changed atmosphere. It seemed like a vacuum, living without the urgent need for total dependency on God. The whole tone of life was changed. I want to let people know it is not always a good thing to have pressure lifted. It can do harm. It can lead to carelessness and take a life away from God-dependency. I cried to God to restore me, and then I took cancer. He allowed this, and it brought me back to the urgency of the need to depend wholly and solely on Him. I had a mastectomy, under which I almost died (I am allergic to anti-biotics, although this was not known at that time). I was expected to be six weeks in hospital, but then something remarkable happened. A young house-doctor who was attending me was obviously surprised that within days the wound was completely dry and there was no discharge. When

*the surgeon arrived, I asked if I could go home, and he gave
me a quizzical look and said, 'Do you think we are miracle
men?' To which I replied, 'I don't think you are a miracle
man, but there is One Who does work miracles.' He looked
at the house doctor, who said. 'Yes, I think she could go
home. The wound is completely healed. There is no
discharge.' To which the surgeon replied, 'Right! home you
go!' I want readers to know it is not always a good thing to
have pressure lifted. It can do harm. There are pressures that
God brings into life that keep us close to God, as did Paul's
thorn in the flesh.*

*In this case God told me that cancer would not recur. He
healed me absolutely and completely. My operation was
about fifteen years ago, and blood tests throughout the period
have proved clear on every occasion, the most recent being a
few months ago. At the time of my operation, God promised
me quite clearly from the Bible that this would not come
upon me a second time. I knew at the time by the reaction
of the doctors that something puzzled them: they could not
understand it. Instead of being discharged in six weeks, I
was out in a week.*

There is a life that springs from death, a strength that
comes from weakness. In my case I have known
desperate weakness, but also times of wonderful Divine
strength. Three times I have been healed, once as
described, once publicly of goitre in my early days—
then much later, when my body was racked with pain,
after long years of suffering. In this case, God came to
me as my Heavenly Father in the night watches, in an
hour of deepest need, when the suffering had become
almost unbearable. He asked me if I wanted to be healed.
I was not free to grasp at this, but said yes, if it was His
Will. Thank God, it was. He touched me, and in a
moment of time I was healed from the crown of my head

to the soles of my feet. The healing was instantaneous and complete—no more migraine, which had been almost chronic; no more intolerable sicknesses—no more general feeling of ill health. From that moment until years later, indeed until I suffered a stroke, I knew what it was to enjoy good health—actually to *enjoy* health. *Instead of merely existing, I began to live.* Perhaps this can only be understood fully by those who have suffered in a similar way.

I believe in healing. I have seen many healed. I have been used in the healing of others. But when I see a servant of God laid aside, I do not judge him or her to be guilty of either hidden sin or lack of faith. Many Christians have been intolerably hurt by such judgments, and have been left with not only their original illness but with a psychological burden as well. Give glory to God when He heals. Give glory to God if you are privileged to go through this particular garden of sorrow and pain for Him, without healing.

In my present situation, the most painful part of my infirmity has been my inability to carry on certain active work for God which was once so dear to me. It has at times been difficult to understand why I have been laid aside when there is so much to do and God is moving so deeply. But God is God, God is sovereign, and the work is God's. All can be safely left in His hands. No man (or woman) is indispensable. God's every goal will be achieved, and it is ours to fit into His perfect plan. We may not always understand, but we can always trust the One Who holds the whole wide world in His hands— Who holds our lives in His hands.

I have wrestled on toward Heaven,
   'Gainst storm, and wind, and tide:

Now, like a weary traveller,
  That leaneth on his guide,
Amid the shades of evening,
  While sinks life's lingering sand,
I hail the glory dawning
  From Immanuel's land.

With mercy and with judgment
  My web of time He wove,
And aye the dews of sorrow
  Were lustred with His love.
I'll bless the hand that guided.
  I'll bless the heart that plann'd,
When throned where glory dwelleth
  In Immanuel's land.

Soon shall the cup of glory
  Wash down earth's bitterest woes,
Soon shall the desert-briar
  Break into Eden's rose:
The curse shall change to blessing –
  The name on earth that's bann'd
Be graven on the white stone
  In Immanuel's land.

His ways are not our ways, His thoughts are not our thoughts, His ways are always best. We live to prove it.

This time of being shut off from human contacts has been a time of being shut in with God, and His reality has been intensified day by day. There is almost an entry into the reality of the eternal presence of God as it shall be.

We write the things we have seen, we speak the things we do know—not just the things we have read about. Personal experience carries great weight.

For my own epitaph, I would like the following lines (adapted from Myers):

Lo, as some venturer from the stars receiving

Promise and presage of sublime emprise
Wears evermore the seal of his believing
Deep in the dark of solitary eyes.

So even I, and with a heart more burning,
So even I, and with a hope more sweet
Yearn for the sign, O Christ, of Thy returning,
Faint for the flaming of Thine advent feet.

[*Author's Note*: Since Miss Taylor's testimony at this point has become very personal, and it is obvious that she herself feels that her days on earth are drawing to a close, it is perhaps appropriate for me to put in my own brief tribute, and give readers some indication of the kind of person she is.

It is difficult to transmit the innerness of one's spiritual impression of another. Perhaps my overriding sense of Miss Taylor is of a person who has had a passionate love for Christ. To her He has been a known personal friend. Around her there is an aura of God which at times has been almost tangible. People tend to come from her presence with a sense not so much of her as of God. Her very room seems full of His presence. I am often reminded of Murray McCheyne, of whom it was said that holiness hung from the walls of his room like a curtain. God's mystical presence has been with her for years. For me she has opened an unusual dimension of God. Almost forty years ago I stood alone on the hills behind Greenock viewing the cemetery and realised even then that in a day to come many would rise to call her blessed. Perhaps my most fitting tribute is simply to say that she transmits God and emanates a peculiar sweetness of Christ. She carries a sense of the mystic and Divine. God has dwelt in her in His power and glory. Glory—

perhaps that is the word—a quality almost indefinable—
but an attribute, a dimension of God Himself.]

23

The Ministry of Women

What shall I add to what Mr. Black has already written on the subject of women ministry in this book? For me the command to pray publicly came from God. The gift of prophecy came from God. The unction to use it came from God. The necessity to preach came from God, although I long resisted the call (and sinfully too, I now believe). God allowed me an Aaron but I may have lacked faith and failed Him here. Through all the years there have been those who have questioned my ministry as a woman and made the work and the work of other ladies in our congregations more difficult—but I never asked to preach or teach, or lay hands on anyone for Baptism in the Spirit, or exorcism, or healing. I sought none of these things:

> How eager is the man to go
> Whom God has never sent,
> How fearful, diffident and slow
> His chosen instrument.

I was a quiet, reserved person who never sought to go into public work. I rebelled. I resisted. 'But God!' Had I acted on my own, men might have shaken me with intellectual arguments. But, you see, I never came that way. I did not start to preach because I thought it was a proper thing for me to do as the result of someone's interpretation of the Bible. I received a call from above. I came under Divine orders and who can gainsay God? Had I been called by man I could have fallen by the way in a day of adversity, but mine was a higher call; the compulsion was Divine and God has fulfilled all that He promised. The intellectual aspect of things is opened up in this book but my convictions need no new book. God settled this for me long ago. I am proud to be numbered with many an 'elect lady' of the past and present. May God bless all my readers and may my ministering daughters (and sons too—I have not forgotten you!) be a mighty host.

NOTE TO READERS

If you would like to enquire further about issues raised in this book or if you feel that the author could be of help you are invited to write to him at 27 Denholm Street, Greenock, PA16 8RH, Scotland, or telephone 0475 87432.

It may also be of interest to know that the author is normally involved in five conferences in Scotland each year— New Year, Easter, July, August and October. Friends gather from many parts of Britain. An open invitation is extended to all and particularly to those interested in the Baptism in the Holy Spirit and related themes. Details will be provided on enquiry.

By the same author

Reflections on the Baptism in the Holy Spirit

The Baptism in the Holy Spirit

- Is it something that happens to us all at conversion, or is it a later and separate experience?
- Should people tarry for it?
- Is it the same as sanctification?
- Do tongues always come with it?
- What about men like Spurgeon and Finney? Did they have this experience?

This book honestly faces many of the problems that the Baptism in the Spirit has raised in the minds of so many in our day. The fact that tens of millions of people now claim to have had this experience, which they describe as similar to what happened to the early disciples on the day of Pentecost, makes the book both topical and relevant.

Published in December 1987, the book has proved very popular and is likely to be used as a textbook on the subject.

£2.25 UK   128pp

By the same author

Reflections on the Gifts of the Spirit

This book speaks of...

- the wonderful operation of the gift of knowledge
- demon exorcism
- miracles of many kinds

Examples are largely drawn from the present day and fall within the personal experience of the author, or of people close to him. Intriguing questions are raised...

- Do demons still speak through human lips?
- Can people receive instantaneous healing?
- Is the future sometimes accurately revealed to God's servants?
- Is angelic ministry real and does it happen today?
- Finally does an ex-Headmaster of a large secondary school, qualified in History (a subject which so often breeds sceptics) believe all these things?

This book is due to be published in March 1988 and contains a number of unusual insights on the gifts in general and on healing, miracles and exorcism in particular.

£2.75 UK   192pp

Reflections on a Song of Love

(A Commentary on 1 Corinthians 13)

First Corinthians Thirteen has a beauty which has enthralled readers through the ages. It highlights Love and reveals attributes of Christ Himself. It has, however, often been used by opponents of pentecostal doctrine—quite wrongly, the author maintains. He raises intriguing questions...

- 'Whether there be tongues, they shall cease'; did this happen with the close of the canon of Scripture?
- Did knowledge cease at the same time? Will knowledge ever cease in this life, and what will replace it in Heaven?
- When Paul became a man he 'put away childish things.' Did this not include tongues?
- Do Christians generally attain the level of Love taught here, and do they display it in their attitudes to each other, as, for example, when these doctrines deeply divide them?

While the main part of this book gives a wonderful description of Christ and the quality of His Love, these controversial issues are not overlooked.

Due for publication in April 1988, this highly original commentary on I Corinthians 13 is likely to attract attention.

£1.25 UK   64pp

Battle for the Body

As in battle rival commanders aim for the same strategic points and seek to exploit each other's weaknesses, so in the spiritual war, where the bodies of men are the battlefield, God and Satan aim to secure control of the same vital centres. Each is interested in areas of weakness – Satan that he may enter and destroy – God that He may guard and strengthen. Satan wants the body to be under his control, obeying his commands and ultimately being possessed by him. God wants the same body that it may be wholly His – a channel for His Spirit: holy, strong and pure.

What are the strategic points round which the battle rages?

- The Head
- The Eyes
- The Ears
- The Tongue
- The Shoulders
- The Heart
- The Hands
- The Knees
- The Backbone
- The Feet

You may be surprised at who really controls these parts of our bodies. Examine the evidence as it is revealed in this searching book.

Due for later publication this book has a practical flavour which will appeal to many.

The Clash of Tongues

(A Commentary on 1 Corinthians 14)

This work deals not only with the regulation of gifts of the Spirit and their relevance for today but also with some of the deeper principles underlying their use. It raises fundamental questions which are sometimes overlooked:

- How can an individual be edified through speaking something which he cannot understand?
- What is the point of speaking in this way when the hearers do not understand either?
- Is there a spiritual means of communication between the human spirit and God which by-passes the intellect and yields benefit?
- Why did Paul have to make regulations at all? If the gifts are Gifts of the Spirit, how can error creep into their use?
- Do the regulations not clash with the direct unctioning of the Spirit upon an individual?
- Tongues according to verse 2 of 1 Corinthians 14 are Godward. Why then is interpretation in modern times so often manward? Surely if God is addressed in one, He will be addressed in the other. Is there Scriptural justification for the present-day practice?
- Was there a difference between the tongues of Acts 2, which were understood by foreigners, and the 'tongues' of 1 Corinthians 14 which 'no man' understood?

These and other points are dealt with as they arise in the text, and it is hoped that both spiritual and intellectual benefit may be derived from the perusal of the solutions offered.

Due for later publication this book, while of general interest, is expected to appeal particularly to serious students of the New Testament.

BOOK ORDERS

The books advertised on the previous pages are being made available to Christian booksellers throughout the country, but if you have any difficulty in obtaining your supply, you may order directly from New Dawn Books, c/o 27 Denholm Street, Greenock, Scotland PA16 8RH.

··············· ORDER FORM ···············

Please send me the books indicated below:

Quantity	Title	Price
	Reflections on the Baptism in the Holy Spirit	£2.25
	Reflections on the Gifts of the Spirit	£2.75
	Reflections on a Song of Love (A commentary on 1 Cor 13)	£1.25
	A Trumpet Call to Women	£2.50
	Consider Him (Twelve Qualities of Christ)	*
	Battle for the Body	*
	The Clash of Tongues (A commentary on 1 Cor 14)	*
	There Shone A Great Light (The Christmas Story)	*

* Prices to be announced

Signature ....

Address ....

....

....

When ordering please send purchase price plus 30p per book to help cover the cost of postage and packaging.